Teresa A. Daniel
Toxic Leaders and Tough Bosses

Teresa A. Daniel

Toxic Leaders and Tough Bosses

Organizational Guardrails to Keep High Performers on Track

DE GRUYTER

ISBN 978-3-11-120110-8
e-ISBN (PDF) 978-3-11-120177-1
e-ISBN (EPUB) 978-3-11-120268-6

Library of Congress Control Number: 2023943021

Bibliographic information published by the Deutsche Nationalbibliothek
The Deutsche Nationalbibliothek lists this publication in the Deutsche Nationalbibliografie;
detailed bibliographic data are available on the internet at http://dnb.dnb.de.

© 2024 Walter de Gruyter GmbH, Berlin/Boston
Cover image: Hybert Design
Typesetting: Integra Software Services Pvt. Ltd.
Printing and binding: CPI books GmbH, Leck

www.degruyter.com

Advance Praise

Toxic and bullying leaders permeate all sectors and organizations, causing billions in lost employee productivity, absenteeism and turnover. In *Toxic Leaders and Tough Bosses: Organizational Guardrails to Keep High-Performers on Track*, Dr. Teresa Daniel delivers a rare achievement: a book that provides background, context and actionable guidance for C-Suite leaders, HR professionals, and supervisors who wish to be tough–effective, yet kind–leaders. Dr. Daniel even provides guidance and recommendations for employees suffering currently under toxic and bullying supervisors. Meticulously referenced with current and relevant research, this book is an authoritative guide and resource for both practitioners and scholars of leadership and human resources.

Anthony A. Piña, Ed.D.
Chief Online Learning Officer
Illinois State University
Editor: *Lessons in Leadership in the Field of Educational Technology* and *Leading and Managing e-Learning: What the e-Learning Leader Needs to Know*

Toxic bosses and the unhealthy work environments they create are a breeding ground for low morale, distrust, and stress. The costs to companies are immense and too often organization leaders are at loss about what to do. They fear losing the "star performer" who gets results and yet causes so much suffering for coworkers. In the meantime, the company's reputation is eroded, talented employees leave for healthier workplaces, and those who stay are distracted, distressed, and feel psychologically unsafe. Finally, here are some answers. In this important book, Dr. Daniel sheds light on the difference between what might be called "tough management", where the leader is demanding but respectful, and abusive leadership, which undermines the wellbeing of employees. Drawing on years of research and experience in the fields of HR management and employment law, *Toxic Leaders and Tough Bosses* provides practical strategies that organizational leaders, HR practitioners, and workplace coaches can take to keep high performers on track, address problems should they arise, and prevent toxicity from occurring in the first place.

Lynn Harrison, PhD
Master Certified Coach, Coaching Supervisor

The timing of *Toxic Leaders and Tough Bosses* comes at such an important time in our society. This book arms the reader with the tools to identify toxic leadership within their organizations and gives ideas and strategies to support employees to create positive workplace cultures. The cost of toxic leaders is high, but the positive impact of great workplace cultures is greater. The choice between the two can make or break an organization. Dr. Daniel paints a clear picture of both. If improving your workplace culture is important to you, then this book is for you!

Charles Gray, MBA, PhD
HR Consultant
U.S. Department of Veterans Affairs

People don't leave jobs, they leave managers. And those managers create toxic workplaces. Toxic leaders permeate the highest ranks of many organizations, and any smart organization must address their destructiveness. *Toxic Leaders and Tough Bosses: Organizational Guardrails to Keep High Performers on Track* offers helpful and much needed guidance to identify and eliminate the toxic leaders that drive away employees and ruin workplaces cultures. The author provides evidence-based strategies and practical tools to encourage organizations to strengthen leaders and managers, creating a positive workplace culture while promoting both respect and high performance. Suggested guardrails help shape leaders and culture, squeezing out toxicity. The valuable roadmap set forth in this book is recommended for Human Resources and all levels of managers and leaders. Its insights offer hope for organizations to turn toxic workplaces into well-functioning, rewarding places of work for all.

Ellen Pinkos Cobb
Attorney & Author of *Managing Psychosocial Hazards and Work-Related Stress in Today's Work Environment*

I highly recommend *Toxic Leaders and Tough Bosses: Organizational Guardrails to Keep High-Performers on Track*. It's a must-read for every leader in a military or traditional business environment. Dr. Teresa Daniel provides a detailed overview of the differences between being a tough boss and being a toxic leader, helps you identify the behaviors that might indicate toxic tendencies, and includes tools for helping you assess and improve your style of leadership. I'm confident that it will inspire you to take an objective look at the way you lead others. If you want to be a better leader, get it – and share it with every leader you know.

Dr. Helen MacLennan
Dean, School of Graduate Business & Technology
Lindsey Wilson College

Dr. Teresa Daniel opens our eyes to the fact that toxic workplaces are destructive–socially, mentally, financially, and even physically. Piercing a veil of delusional normalcy, beyond which workplace cultures themselves honor, endorse – and even reward – erstwhile exploitation of our common emotional biology, she arms us with pragmatic science-based solutions that serve everyone's best interest. To survive, to thrive . . . read this book!

Katherine Peil Kauffman
Interdisciplinary Emotion Theorist and Director, EFS International

Army leadership is a delicate balance between "tough love" and building a trustworthy relationship with those you will lead into the most difficult environment young men and women will ever face--combat. Toxic leaders cannot build the trust, respect and loyalty that it takes. There is no place in any organization for toxic leaders, but especially not in the US Army. Leaders must understand the detrimental effect and impact that toxic leadership has on building the necessary respect and trust for their important mission supporting our great country. Hopefully, the US Army and organizations across the globe will require this book as mandatory reading and use it as a foundation in their leadership programs to teach and build competent, caring and tough leaders while continuing to weed out the bullies and toxic leaders.

Brigadier General James E. Shane,
US Army (Ret)

Contents

The Impact of a Toxic Organizational Culture: Why Should You Care?

Leadership Changes Everything: Types of Leaders and How They Impact Employees and Their Organizations

Organizational Toxicity: Factors Which Promote Toxic Behavior

HR's Role in the Management of Organizational Culture and Employee Well-Being

Evidence-Based Strategies: Building Stronger Organizational Cultures

Strategies and Tools: Developing Better Leaders and Managers

Building the Future of Work

Appendices

Dedication

Billions of wasted dollars. Millions of miserable people. It's not a warzone—it's the state of the American workplace. Toxicity itself isn't new. But now that we know the high costs and how managers can make workplaces better, there's no excuse for inaction.

~ Johnny C. Taylor, CEO of SHRM (2019)

If your organization has toxic stars, you don't just have a culture problem. You also have a broken reward system. In healthy organizations, the impact people have on others is a key factor in their pay, performance, and promotions. If you're an asshole, you're not a success.

~ Adam Grant, Organizational Psychologist (2022)

It is my hope that the collective good work of dedicated leaders, managers, researchers, scholars, practitioners, and activists will someday result in fewer toxic leaders and more organizations that simply refuse to tolerate them—regardless of their ability to deliver results.

The available research unequivocally confirms that creating and sustaining a positive workplace climate—one based on honesty, integrity, fairness, dignity, and respect for all employees—is not just the right thing to do, it is also a business imperative. I couldn't agree more. This book is dedicated to a future where that goal is realized.

References

Society for Human Resource Management (2019, September 25). *Press release*. https://www.shrm.org/about-shrm/press-room/press-releases/pages/shrm-reports-toxic-workplace-cultures-cost-billions.aspx.
Grant, A. (October 19, 2022). *LinkedIn*. https://www.linkedin.com/feed/update/urn:li:activity:6986685844698886144/.

https://doi.org/10.1515/9783111201771-203

Foreword

At its core, the role of human resource (HR) professionals is the care and management of organizational relationships. How easy or difficult that role is to fulfill depends on the nature of the relationships involved. There are organizations in which every individual employee matters. Think of a small family business, or an equally small company for which the identity and reputation are ultimately the sum of the skills and capacities of the people who work there. Every product, or job, or interaction matters.

Contrast that with an organization, typically much larger, where the majority of the jobs are functionally automated. They may still be filled by humans, but it seems to make little difference which humans fill them. If the jobs could be done by a machine, at equal or lower cost, the owners would gladly make the change.

Neither of these extremes is inherently right or wrong. How functional they are in a given situation largely depends on the leaders of the organization and the nature of the work. Importantly, though, the culture that gets established is rarely done with foresight and intention. It is often an unconscious reflection of people and circumstances.

Think of a small startup company built on the ideas of the founder, possibly a technical genius. The company adds people only because the work gets bigger than the founder can handle, and she sees the need to grow the business. In this case, the roles of employees are considered necessary, but only in functional ways.

By contrast, consider a specialty boutique (products or services), where individual care and attention of customers is paramount. A couple of bad interactions, particularly with high-profile or influential patrons, could significantly damage the brand. Every employee is important because they create the interactions, and you wouldn't think of putting those relationships in the hands of someone that you couldn't trust.

These two examples are purposefully extreme, but they represent tensions found across many workplaces. The most important question which emerges is, "What is the value of employees to *that* organization?" When you can answer that question, you'll have a good start on deciding how difficult the potential HR role is likely to be.

The HR role itself usually arises in a given context. It could be, "I really need someone to help me build the right team to get this venture going. That will make or break its future success." Alternately, it could be that the organization simply got big enough to need someone to handle hiring, payroll and benefits. And from there, the HR role grew as needed. Again, the differences are not inherently right or wrong, but they can be devastating to the success of an organization if there is a mismatch between the needs and skills of an organization.

There are no human prerequisites for starting an organization. No one has to pass a test. A free enterprise system lets each entrepreneur succeed or fail according to their own efforts and luck.

Some people have exceptionally adept skills with other people, knowing how to understand them, foreseeing problems, dealing with conflicts and even helping them develop through their careers. Other people simply don't start with those skills, or

https://doi.org/10.1515/9783111201771-204

only with very limited versions of them. In some cases, it works out. If an organization can succeed based purely on technical prowess or cost-driven transactions, human issues might cause minimal damage. In other cases, the human toll erodes the foundation of the organization itself, and eventually destroys it with little understanding of what happened.

This applies to supervisors and managers as much as it does to owners and executives. Some organizations still provide at least minimal training for new supervisors, but many organizations have redirected those investments to new technologies instead. There is no necessary core of human or relational expertise required.

In reality, though, there are very few organizations where people make little to no difference. There are cases where the feedback loops are long and delayed—places where attention to the well-being of employees is virtually non-existent. In the meantime, the toll on employees who unknowingly wander through its ranks, simply needing employment, can be devastating. For those, we should probably require hazardous warning signs on the employment ads.

HR professionals rarely get to choose the nature of the relationships that they will face in a given organization. There may be hints or indications, but unless you are intimately familiar with an organization in advance, skeletons remain hidden in closets until a crisis or conflict brings them out.

As noted in this book, HR professionals work for the organization. They carry significant responsibilities to support individual employees too, but in the end, their ultimate responsibilities are to the organizations who employ them. That can create unresolvable tensions, especially in the face of truly toxic leaders who are often legally and financially in control.

In the hardest situations, HR professionals have to make choices about their own well-being. When you determine that you are facing the impossible, I hope you will choose yourself, your health, and your moral integrity. There are workplace situations and people in the current reality that you simply cannot fix, no matter how much you care.

This book addresses many of the challenges that organizations often face and offers examples and suggestions for dealing with them. It is written by an author who worked as an employment law attorney in a major corporation and who has conducted research and taught for many years as the dean of a program focused on HR leadership at an American university. In those roles, she has faced many of the problems she outlines in this book.

There is still much to be done to create the kind of positive organizational cultures discussed in this book—places where employees can show up to do their best work—but it is possible to get closer to that goal than where we are now. Organizational leaders, managers, supervisors, and HR practitioners are the primary drivers for these important workplace changes and there are many hopeful signs to suggest that you are collectively making a real difference.

Gary S. Metcalf, PhD
President, InterConnections LLC
Dr. Metcalf is the co-author of *Stop Bullying at Work: Strategies and Tools for HR, Legal & Risk Management Professionals* (SHRM, 2016) and *The Management of People in Mergers & Acquisitions* (Quorum Books, 2001). He is the founder and President of InterConnections, LLC, a management consulting company focused on resolving complex workplace issues related to human capital.

Preface

Guardrails are tools used to ensure that employees and company leaders are aligned with the organization's goals and objectives. They also help to keep people from unintentionally straying into dangerous territory at work. When well-conceived, guardrails consist of strong organizational values, clear behavioral expectations, and fair and comprehensive policies, procedures, and reward structures. They include an unwavering expectation that all people will be treated with respect and dignity, and an assurance of accountability for those who do not honor these expectations.

Much like guardrails along the roadway keep drivers safer and on track to reach their end destination, organizational guardrails help to protect individuals from taking misguided shortcuts or wrong turns by clearly defining boundaries for the trickiest areas they are likely to encounter along the way.

In this book you will find numerous ideas about how you can implement the types of guardrails that are most likely to help your toxic leaders and tough bosses perform at their peak capacity while minimizing their negative impact on both employees and the organization. It will require careful planning and an intense focus on accountability—the kind that requires both employees and leaders to focus not just on results, but also on the way that results are actually accomplished.

All in all, the intended result of this book is that you and your organization can use the knowledge and tools discussed in the pages ahead to realize as many of its aspirational goals as possible while becoming the success it is meant to be.

https://doi.org/10.1515/9783111201771-205

About This Book

Although no single resource can provide all of the answers, this book is designed to serve as a roadmap which will guide you—whether you are an organizational leader, mid-level manager, supervisor, or an HR/OD practitioner—as you work to cultivate a culture that promotes high-performance while also valuing fairness, respect, and accountability for all employees.

As described in this book, "toxic high performers" are those individuals who consistently achieve stellar results. They have impressive credentials and off-the-chart talent, but because of their behaviors toward others, their unchecked ego, or their lack of sensitivity, they end up ripping organizations apart. How? Because they cannot keep a staff and the organization suffers because good people leave, knowing that they can do better someplace else. Or they consistently denigrate employees which causes the team to be less than it otherwise could be.

Make no mistake—toxic leaders are often brilliant superstars who invariably meet or exceed their performance targets—after all, that's why they are often called "stars". However, their behavior is often so abominable that people refuse to work with them, ultimately deciding to "vote with their feet" and leave your organization. Worse yet, they stay but feel demeaned, bullied, and unable to perform at their best due to the climate of fear the toxic leader creates in their force-field.

Although toxic stars are often widely known to be bullies, jerks, or assholes, they are often treated as if they are "untouchable" due to their incredible results, meaning that they are frequently coddled and treated as if the rules which apply to the rest of us do not apply to them. As a result, they have the power to create and sustain a hostile work environment which negatively impacts employee morale and lowers overall team performance. It also results in higher levels of attrition.

The truth is that we need people in our organizations who can get results; however, left unchecked, toxic stars can be a cancer on a company's culture. Toxic leaders need to learn that if they act like a jerk or, worse yet, are widely perceived by their colleagues to be "a full-fledged asshole", they are not going to continue to be successful. Period. Full stop—end of discussion—regardless of their results.

As Adam Grant (an organizational psychologist at The Wharton School of Business) and many others have noted, in healthy organizations, "the impact people have on others is a key factor in their pay, performance, and promotions" (Grant, 2022). If they continue to be rewarded or promoted despite their abusive behavior toward others, employees are left with the inescapable conclusion that their company values profits over its people, regardless of the values it proclaims to hold dear.

To give you a sense of what will be covered in the pages ahead, here is a snapshot of the topics that will be examined by chapter:

In Chapter 1 we discuss the signs of a toxic workplace and take a look at recent surveys and reports in order to "take the temperature" of our workplaces. The result is dismal: we are collectively not doing very well at all. In Chapter 2, we will examine

https://doi.org/10.1515/9783111201771-206

some of the history which has led us to this time when toxic leaders are so prevalent and our workplaces are so brutal.

Then in Chapter 3 we will take a look at the types of leaders you most commonly have to deal with—ranging from tough to toxic—and we will closely examine the impact that toxic leaders have on organizational culture and employee well-being.

We will then focus our attention on the characteristics that turn a good leader into an exceptional one in Chapter 4. Spoiler alert: there really are many exceptional leaders in organizations throughout the world who treat their people with respect and who are doing extraordinary things for both their companies and for their employees. While we more frequently hear about the bad ones in sensational news stories about imploding careers, it is my hope that you will find this chapter to be uplifting—and maybe even inspiring.

In Chapter 5 we will turn our attention to some of the societal influences that conspire to develop the toxic leaders who show up in our workplaces, along with some practical ideas about how we might meet these challenges.

Context matters. Toxic leaders cannot thrive in a culture which does not allow them to do so—what is often referred to as a "conducive climate" (also known as a lack of accountability). Factors that conspire to create an environment where organizational toxicity can thrive will be discussed at length in Chapter 6.

Then Chapter 7 will examine the dangerous ethical crossroad that occurs when senior leaders are at the peak of their careers. It is at that time when their egos are often at their most expansive due to their organizational success. It is also the time when they have the least guardrails and oversight—the time they are most likely to become toxic, make serious ethical mistakes, and cross over to "the dark side".

HR practitioners have an enormous impact on policies and procedures, and they are almost always front-and-center when it comes to managing pay and reward processes. These systems help to set the tone of the organization which allows toxic leaders to either thrive or be pushed out. Because of HR's significance in driving the organization's culture, the critical role of practitioners will be examined in Chapter 8, while evidence-based strategies HR can use to help employees cope with difficult bosses are outlined in Chapter 9.

Chapter 10 focuses on the performance-conduct circle. This model is based on the premise that results are just a part of the overall equation and that how those results are achieved should be an important part of the decision making when it comes to an individual's pay and promotions. It will make the case about why even off-the-charts performance should not be allowed to justify toxic behavior—the ultimate cost for everyone involved is just too high.

In Chapter 11 the focus will be on how to build and sustain a positive workplace culture by considering the concept of "guardrails"—mutually enforcing organizational policies and expectations designed to keep high performers in check and on the right path. It is my hope that these evidence-based strategies will give you a broad range of options to consider so that you can develop customized solutions that will work best for your organization.

Some of the potential danger zones—where critical policies, procedures, and reward structures are needed to help your company minimize organizational toxicity and avoid legal liability—will be examined in Chapter 12.

In Chapter 13 we will identify the components of an effective management and supervisory development program, while Chapter 14 provides some practical tools that you can use to help develop more self-awareness among your high performers. The goal here is to provide some exercises that can be used in your training workshops to help strengthen your leaders and managers so that they can be ready to help take your company to the next level.

Chapter 15 will outline an idealized design for a positive organizational culture—one where most all of us would actually want to go to work every day. Who knows? Maybe it will provide the inspiration needed to take your organization to the next level! And finally, in Chapter 16 we will review some of the events in recent years that suggest hopeful signs for the future of our workplaces, both in the U.S. and worldwide.

The inspiration for this book is based on empirical research involving senior officers in the U.S. Army stationed at bases in Ft. Leavenworth, Kansas and Ft. Knox, Kentucky. An overview of the design of this foundational study is included in *Appendix I*, while an executive summary of the findings as they relate to toxic leaders and tough bosses is included in *Appendix II*. The findings about exceptional leaders can be found in *Appendix III*. Lastly, *Appendix IV* includes comments from study participants describing the great leaders they have been fortunate to have been led by. I hope you find them to be as inspirational as I do! Unless noted to the contrary, the italic quotations used throughout this book are excerpted from these studies.

The book is structured in a linear fashion so that it can be read straight through, but feel free to skip ahead to the chapters in which you have a more pressing interest if that suits your available time or current need for information. Note also that while the foundational research occurred in the United States, toxic leaders are present (and prevalent) in workplaces everywhere. Efforts have been made to include global examples where they serve to provide additional insight or clarity.

Turn the page and we will begin to explore some of the differences between toxic high performers and exceptionally tough bosses. We will also cover a wide variety of strategies that can be used to keep them productive and contributing to the organization's bottom line, while at the same time holding them accountable for their impact on those in their path.

The ultimate goal is to help high performers understand that while getting results is certainly appreciated and of great value to the organization, it is only *part* of the equation. They must also collaborate, communicate, and mentor others in order to create a positive workplace climate for all of your employees and the potential for long-term viability and success for the organization.

The road ahead is most assuredly not easy. After all, if it were, anyone could do it—and it is a pretty solid bet that your organization is counting on *you* to lead the way.

Reference

Grant, A. (2022, October 19). *LinkedIn.* https://www.linkedin.com/feed/?trk=hb_tab_home_top.

Acknowledgements

The author wishes to thank her husband and colleague, **Dr. Gary Metcalf**, for his partnership on the study of toxic leaders within the U.S. Army which is foundational to this book. His contributions were significant—from the earliest conceptualization of the study's design, to the collection and analysis of the data, and concluding with the writing of this book's *Foreword*. He frequently operates as a critical thought partner on my research and writing projects while continuing to be my best and most trusted friend, collaborator, and life partner.

Many thanks to **Dr. Helen MacLennan** who served as the principal research assistant on the project. There was no doubt back then that she would become an outstanding scholar-practitioner—and she has!

A heartfelt thanks also to **Stephen Metcalf** and **Marigail Sexton** for their wise insights and contributions to the chapter about the societal issues that influence individuals to become toxic leaders and the factors that embolden them to adopt workplace behaviors that negatively affect both employees and their organizations.

In addition, the author is grateful to **Sullivan University** for the generous faculty grant which provided funding for the research study about toxic leaders which inspired this book, as well as for their unwavering support, funding, and recognition of her research efforts over the course of many years.

The author also wishes to express her sincere gratitude to **Brigadier General James Shane (Ret)** for his enthusiasm for the project and for the introductions that he provided. Without his unwavering support, the foundational research for this book would likely not have happened.

Finally, the author wishes to express her gratitude to the **U.S. Army officers** from bases at both Ft. Knox, Kentucky and Ft. Leavenworth, Kansas who generously took the time to be interviewed for the research study. Both individually and as a collective group, they were articulate, thoughtful, smart, and impressive by any measure. Without them, the original research study leading to this book would not have been possible.

https://doi.org/10.1515/9783111201771-207

The Impact of a Toxic Organizational Culture: Why Should You Care?

Chapter 1
Toxic Workplace Cultures Hurt Employees and Reduce Company Profits

What keeps you up at night or causes you to dread going in to work the next morning? For way too many of us, that answer is a toxic workplace culture or working for a destructive leader, or worse yet, both. There is now unequivocal evidence to support why so many experience the "Sunday scaries"—that yucky, anxious feeling in the pit of your stomach as the weekend is winding down, or really just any time that you think about heading into the office (Pandise, 2017).

The word "toxic" comes from the Greek "toxikon" which means "arrow poison". In a literal sense, the term in its original form means to kill (poison) in a targeted way (arrow). Destructive leaders are described as toxic because they are, indeed, poisonous to one's spirit. Over time, the buildup of this toxicity leaves affected employees feeling devalued, demoralized, and often hopeless. Nothing good ever results from toxic anything.

Research from the Society for Human Resource Management (SHRM, 2019), the largest HR professional association in the United States, reports that toxic workplace cultures have driven 20% of U.S. employees out of their jobs in the past five years—at a turnover cost greater than $223 billion! Yes, you read that right. A toxic work culture drives away 1 in 5 employees and comes with an annual $44.6 billion-dollar cost to American organizations.

SHRM's report, *The High Cost of a Toxic Workplace Culture*, surveyed American workers to explore the impact of workplace culture on both their well-being and the bottom line of businesses. This report described toxic workplaces as work environments where employees dread going to work, do not feel they can be honest with their manager, and may witness or experience sexual harassment or age discrimination (SHRM, 2019).

Bad bosses are common in organizations across the world, despite the reported $166 billion annual spending on leadership development in the U.S. alone (Westfall, 2019). Toxic workplace cultures are, in large part, created by toxic people who engage in aggressive actions, micromanage, and operate in ways that undermine trust and loyalty. These behaviors can be *indirect*, taking the form of hostile jokes and teasing and/or undermining the work and accomplishment of others. Toxic behaviors can be *direct* as well. Shouting, ridicule, excessive criticism, bullying, and scapegoating are all hallmarks of a toxic company culture.

When an organization's culture is truly toxic, trust, a sense of psychological safety, and employee morale are degraded to unhealthy levels and employees suffer from emotional and physical exhaustion, conflict between work and family, high levels of anxiety and stress, lack of sleep, and even psychological distress. In a nutshell,

https://doi.org/10.1515/9783111201771-001

everyone loses. Conversely, there is a strong correlation between a positive workplace culture, satisfied and engaged employees, and business productivity and profits (Workhuman, 2019; National Business Research Institute, n.d.; Kusy & Holloway, 2009).

SHRM's report found that toxic cultures create "astronomical" costs to organizations in terms of turnover and absenteeism. In fact, this report noted that the cost of productivity loss due to unplanned absences is approximately $431 billion per year, with up to $86 billion per year attributed to employees calling in sick when they just don't feel like going to work. In addition, the report highlighted common indicators of bad workplace cultures (such as discrimination and harassment) and it underscored the alarming impact that a negative environment has on employees.

Toxicity can manifest itself in many ways at work, including sexual harassment and discriminatory treatment such as ageism or racism. It is commonly the result of an individual with a toxic personality—meaning those people who demonstrate a pattern of counterproductive work behaviors that cause harm to their employees, teams, or organization over the long term.

SHRM's findings are consistent with an extensive body of management literature that reports between 65 percent to 75 percent of employees believe their boss to be the worst part of their jobs, as well as voluminous other research which links toxicity to decreased employee well-being (exhibited most frequently as physical illness, including chronic stress, anger and anxiety, coronary disease, asthma, diabetes, and arthritis), as well as lower performance (Gallup Organization, 2015; Lombardo & McCall, 1984).

Although this book draws heavily on organizational research and data generated in the U.S., employees throughout the world are experiencing similar problems at work. More than two decades ago now, countries in the European Union began to address the issue of workplace bullying and mobbing through laws and regulations designed to protect employees from such abuse while at work (Hoel, 2018). Voluminous research confirms that toxicity at work is a problem of global magnitude, occurring in both advanced and emerging nations (Rasool, Wang, Tang, Saeed, & Iqbal, 2021).

There is no doubt about it. Organizations across the globe are not functioning well, especially when it comes to the management of their human capital. In fact, it is probably an understatement to describe them as a "hot mess" despite the fact that smart, educated, and (theoretically) capable people hold most senior organizational positions. The situation begs this question then: why is it so complicated for people to lead with kindness and simply treat others the way that they want to be treated?

Key Findings From the Study

SHRM notes its key findings from the study as follows:
- Only 38% of American employees are "very satisfied" with their current job;

- 49% have thought about leaving their current organization;
- 1 in 5 (20%) have left a job due to workplace culture;
- 58% of those who left a job due to culture claim that their manager is the reason they ultimately left;
- 25% of Americans define organizational culture as a combination of employees' attitudes, actions, and behaviors;
- 76% say their manager sets the culture of their workplace;
- 36% say their manager doesn't know how to lead a team;
- 1 in 4 (25%) dread going to work, don't feel safe voicing their opinions about work-related issues; and don't feel respected and valued at work; and
- 4 in 10 say their manager fails to frequently engage in honest conversations about work topics.

Also noteworthy was the finding that employees hold their workplace managers directly responsible for creating the toxicity—more than either senior leaders or HR. Moreover, 58 percent of employees (6 in 10) who quit a job due to culture indicated that their manager is the main reason that they ultimately left.

What are these managers doing that is so wrong? SHRM's research identified what appears to be a critical skills gap at the management level. While managers are in a prime position to build strong and positive climates by listening to employees, holding them accountable for their actions, setting expectations, and clarifying information, apparently the perception among employees is that they are not executing these duties very well at all.

In addition to ineffective managerial skills, the report suggested that a failure to communicate openly and transparently is a leading contributor to the culture issues facing many organizations. Sadly, nearly 25 percent of employees said they do not feel safe voicing their opinions about work-related issues, nor do they feel respected and valued at work. Bad leaders are toxic in every sense of the term and their impact frequently spills over to their friends and family, with 33 percent reporting that workplace culture makes them irritable at home.

Some of the Top Signs of a Toxic Workplace

There is a growing body of research that has examined this problem in great detail. Their findings are dismal, but fairly consistent. According to Workhuman (2019), the top ten signs of a toxic workplace include:
- Insufficient or dishonest communication;
- Failure of managers to listen;
- Lack of recognition of good work;
- Performance appraisals that are too negative;
- Rampant office politics;

– Bullying;
– Discrimination;
– Sexual harassment;
– Expectations that employees will take ethically or legally questionable actions; and
– Disrespect for work/life balance.

Similarly, in a 2023 study, *Culture Fitness: Healthy Habits of High-Performance Organizations*, i4cp (in partnership with *HR Executive*), examined the characteristics of both healthy and unhealthy cultures (i4cp & HR Executive, 2023). They found nine common habits consistently cited by organizations with what they referred to as "unfit cultures".
    Labeled "the toxic 9", they include these types of persistent workplace characteristics:
– Bureaucratic;
– Non-inclusive;
– Disrespectful;
– Chaotic;
– Complacent;
– Cut-throat;
– Hierarchical;
– Insensitive; and
– Conflict avoidant.

In an era where productivity is waning, the study also found that cultural fitness is directly linked to productivity. In fact, regression analysis revealed that culture health explained nearly 20% of increased organizational productivity over the past two years.
    The immense impact on productivity plus the price tag to American companies of a staggering $223 billion over the past five years should be more than enough to convince your senior leadership that tackling the issue of a toxic culture is a problem worthy of their attention and resources. That is an enormous number of misdirected resources that could be spent in other more productive ways. Modeling the way and imposing accountability for those leaders who cannot (or will not) change will allow a positive climate to take root and continue to grow.

The Current State of American Organizations

If what you have read so far has not yet convinced you that we have a problem of crisis proportion in our workplaces, read on. These additional studies are dismal, suggesting that employees are disengaged, do not trust their leaders, and in many cases are simply checked out.

MIT Sloan Management Review Study (2022)

According to a recent report from the MIT Sloan Management Review, employees are quitting "in droves" because of toxic workplace culture, not low pay (Sull, Sull, Cipolli, & Brighenti, 2022). In fact, the report concludes that a toxic workplace culture is 10.4 times more likely to contribute to employee resignations than compensation.

Five attributes of an organization's perceived culture have, by far, the largest negative impact on how employees rate their work environment. These include workplaces that are perceived by employees as:
- Disrespectful (lack of consideration, courtesy, and dignity for others);
- Non-inclusive (inequities related to LGBTQ, disability, racial bias, age, gender, cronyism and nepotism, and generally non-inclusive); and
- Unethical (prevalence of unethical behavior, dishonesty, and lack of regulatory compliance);
- "Cut-throat" (e.g., backstabbing behavior and ruthless competition); and
- "Abusive" (a high prevalence of bullying, harassment, and hostility).

The 2021 Workplace Bullying Institute (WBI) U.S. Workplace Bullying Survey

In the latest national survey, 30% of Americans reported that they have suffered abusive conduct at work defined by WBI as "repeated mistreatment: abusive conduct that is threatening, intimidating, humiliating, work sabotage or verbal abuse". Another 19% have witnessed it—that's 79.3 million American workers who are affected by workplace bullying, both directly and indirectly. The target of bullying is female in 49% of all cases, while 67% of all bullies are men. Targets typically do not report the situation and when they do, 60% received a negative reaction from their employer who faulted them for their "ineffective reactions" (Workplace Bullying Institute, 2021).

SHRM State of the Workplace Study 2021–2022

SHRM's most recent *State of the Workplace Study* identified "maintaining employee morale and engagement" as their highest priority for 2022 (SHRM, 2022). Prior surveys indicated that only 44 percent of American employees feel extremely or very fulfilled in their current job. What this means is that more than half of all employees—56 percent—feel less than fulfilled at work. These findings are a pretty stark indictment of the current state of our workplaces, and I think we can all agree that it is most definitely not looking too good (SHRM, 2019)!

American Psychological Association 2023 Work In America Survey and 2022 Work and Well-Being Survey

Findings of the American Psychological Association (APA) are similarly dismal. Employees apparently do not feel valued and they do not trust their leaders (American Psychological Association, 2022; American Psychological Association, 2014). The APA report noted that employees who do not feel valued are less likely to be engaged in their work, have lower levels of energy, higher levels of stress, and report lower levels of job satisfaction, among other findings.

In the APA's 2023 Work in America Survey, 19% of those surveyed said that their workplace is "very" or "somewhat" toxic. Those who reported working in a toxic environment were more than 3 times likely to have said that they have experienced harm to their mental health at work than those who report working in a healthy workplace (52% vs 15%) (American Psychological Association, 2023).

Gallup Survey on Employee Engagement 2022

The Gallup Organization regularly surveys employees about how engaged they feel, defining engaged employees as "those who are involved in, enthusiastic about and committed to their work and workplace". Only about a third of those surveyed reported being engaged at work (Gallup Organization, 2023; Harter & Adkins, 2015).

This finding has remained fairly consistent since 2000 when Gallup first began measuring and reporting on U.S. workplace engagement—until now. Gallup's latest report indicates that engagement has reached its lowest level in nine years. Only 32 percent of the employees surveyed responding that they felt engaged in their work and 18 percent reported that they were "actively disengaged" (Gallup Organization, 2015).

Gallup's report indicated that the engagement elements with the steepest declines were:
– Clarity of expectations;
– Connection to the mission or purpose of the company;
– Opportunities to learn and grow;
– Opportunities to do what employees do best; and
– Feeling cared about at work.

These issues are not U.S.-centric, either. According to Gallup's report, disengaged employees cost the world $7.8 trillion a year in lost productivity. Astonishingly, that is equal to about 11 percent of global GDP (Gallup Organization, 2023)!

Sadly, a majority of employees currently working in organizations throughout the world are apparently "indifferent, sleepwalking through their workday without regard for their performance or their organization's performance" (Gallup Organization, 2023).

The "So What"

The research confirms that employees are not really engaged in their jobs and the current way our organizations are managed and structured is simply not working for them. The result is a prevalence of toxic cultures that suck the joy out of work. If employees are not engaged in their jobs and feel demoralized when they walk through your organization's front door, then it stands to reason that there will be a significantly negative impact on vital business outcomes such as profitability and productivity.

All of the data suggests that the payoff of an improved culture can be absolutely huge—and it's not rocket science. Frequent and honest communication, showing appreciation, recognizing good work, being inclusive, and treating employees fairly and with respect will create a greater sense of trust, belonging, commitment, and engagement. It will also allow employees to do more than just come to work and pick up a paycheck; it will cause them to personally and professionally thrive and flourish while contributing to your organization's long-term success (SHRM Foundation, 2016).

Importantly, though, implementing these changes is, at most, just *partly* your responsibility. Senior leaders must also be actively involved in setting your company's culture strategy and by setting the "tone at the top" that enforces the new ways of operating. According to SHRM's report:

> True culture change occurs when it becomes a shared responsibility among workplace decision makers.

Make no mistake, HR can influence behavior and make a hugely positive difference to both employees and to the organization—but not by working solo. When it comes to workplace culture, the buck stops at the door of the C-suite.

References

American Psychological Association (2014). *Employer distrust is pervasive in U.S. workforce*. https://www.apa.org/news/press/releases/2014/04/employee-distrust.

American Psychological Association (2022). *APA 2022 Work and Well-Being Survey*. https://www.apa.org/pubs/reports/work-well-being/2022-mental-health-support.

American Psychological Association (2023). *Work in America Survey*. https://www.apa.org/pubs/reports/work-in-america/2023-workplace-health-well-being.

Gallup Organization (2015). *State of the American manager: Analytics and advice for leaders*. https://www.gallup.com/services/182138/state-american-manager.aspx.

Gallup Organization (2023, January 25). *Gallup 2022 Survey on Employee Engagement*. https://www.gallup.com/workplace/468233/employee-engagement-needs-rebound-2023.aspx.

Grant, A. (2022, October 19). *LinkedIn*. https://www.linkedin.com/feed/?trk=hb_tab_home_top.

Harter, J. & Adkins, A. (2015, April 8). Employees want a lot more from their managers. *Gallup*. https://www.gallup.com/workplace/236570/employees-lot-managers.aspx.

Hoel, H. (2018). Study: Bullying and sexual harassment at the workplace, in public spaces, and political life in the EU. https://www.europarl.europa.eu/thinktank/en/document/IPOL_STU(2018)604949.

i4cp and HR Executive (2023). *Culture fitness: Healthy habits of high-performance organizations*. https://hrexecutive.com/new-year-new-you-new-organizational-culture/?oly_enc_id= 4791B7303167C6Y.

Kusy, M. & Holloway, E. (2009). *Toxic workplace! Managing toxic personalities and their systems of power*. Jossey-Bass.

Lombardo, M.M. & McCall, M.W. J. (1984). *Coping with an intolerable boss*. Center for Creative Leadership.

National Business Research Institute (n.d.). *The high price of a toxic company culture*. https://www.nbrii. com/blog/high-price-toxic-company-culture/.

Pandise, E. (2017, July 16). The "Sunday Scaries" are real—Here's why. *NBC News*. https://www.nbcnews. com/better/health/sunday-scaries-are-real-why-ncna783186.

Rasool, S.F., Wang, M., Tang, M., Saeed, A. & Iqbal, J. (2021). How toxic workplace environment effects the employee engagement: The mediating role of organizational support and employee wellbeing. *International Journal of Environmental Research and Public Health*, *18*, 2294. https://doi.org/10.3390/ ijerph1052294.

SHRM Foundation (2016). *Creating a more human workplace where employees and businesses thrive*. https://www.shrm.org/hr-today/trends-and-forecasting/special-reports-and-expert-views/Docu ments/Human-Workplace.pdf.

Society for Human Resource Management (2019). *The high cost of a toxic workplace culture: How culture impacts the workforce—and the bottom line*. https://pages.shrm.org/2019culturereport?_ga=2. 46299751.1379352704.1569245079-1873814319.1519658911.

Society for Human Resource Management (2022). *State of the Workplace Report 2021–2022*. https://www. shrm.org/hr-today/trends-and-forecasting/research-and-surveys/Pages/SHRM-State-of-the-Workplace-Report-.aspx.

Sull, D., Sull, C., Cipolli, W. & C. Brighenti (2022, March 22). Why every leader needs to worry about toxic culture. *MIT Sloan Management Review*. https://sloanreview.mit.edu/article/why-every-leader-needs-to -worry-about-toxic-culture/.

Westfall, C. (2019, June 20). Leadership development is a $366 billion industry: Here's why most programs don't work. *Forbes*. https://www.forbes.com/sites/chriswestfall/2019/06/20/leadership-development-why-most-programs-dont-work/#235cbacd61de.

Workhuman (2019, October 30). *The cost of toxic cultures*. https://www.workhuman.com/resources/globo force-blog/the-cost-of-toxic-cultures.

Workplace Bullying Institute (WBI) 2021 U.S. Workplace Bullying Study (2021, February 23). https://workplacebullying.org/2021-wbi-survey/.

Chapter 2
Some Historical Context: How We Got Here

Context and history are key to understanding the complex world in which we currently live and work. Why does it seem that toxic individuals have become so prevalent in our organizations as well as in society at large? How did we get here? Spoiler alert: it did not happen overnight. Some of the issues that have combined and accelerated over the last three decades to create the type of conducive work environments in which toxic leaders can thrive will be examined next.

A Relentless Focus on the Maximization of Profits

In a highly influential *New York Times* essay written by Milton Friedman (1970), he contended that "the (only) responsibility of business is to maximize profits". With limited exceptions, there has been widespread acceptance of his view since that time. Corporations obviously need to achieve results and be profitable, but that is only a *part* of their responsibility. They also are responsible for maximizing all of their assets, including people. As noted by Kenneth Mason, quoted in Makower (2006):

> The moral imperative all of us share in this world is that of getting the best return we can on whatever assets we are privileged to employ. What American business leaders too often forget is that this means all the assets employed—not just the financial assets but also the brains employed, the labor employed, the materials employed, and the land, air, and water employed.

Fueled by activist shareholders, private-equity firms, and bonuses based on stock prices, it seems that corporate leaders instead are obsessed with maximizing quarterly profits—and they have been quite successful in doing so. Institutional investors have also had great influence on corporate decision making in recent years. They believe that caring about anything but profits is inappropriate. Interestingly, some have even suggested that any other focus is even possibly a violation of management's fiduciary responsibility (Greider, 2009). As a result of this short-term focus, many companies fail to adequately consider the interests of their other key stakeholders: customers, employees, society, and the planet.

The result is a de-humanizing of the workplace. It has become a place where people are often treated badly and managers are rewarded for those very behaviors. As noted by Edwards (1996, p. 163):

> The forbidden truth is that we are living by a set of lies which are necessary for short-term profit, at the expense of human, physical, and psychological life and global environmental integrity. We are living in a system where power ensures that the requirements of profit take priority over the requirements of living things [. . .]. Consequently our freedom extends as far as, and no further

https://doi.org/10.1515/9783111201771-002

than, the satisfaction of these requirements, with all else being declared neurosis, paranoia, communism, extremism, the work of the devil, or Neptunian nonsense.

This profit obsession has created significant changes for employees over the last thirty years. It is these changes that we will examine next.

Changes in the Workplace

In the past, working for a corporation was significantly defined by promises. Corporations committed to provide employees with lifetime job security, fair compensation, health care, and a secure retirement plan. In exchange, employees promised to show up every day, perform their work, and be loyal to the organization. Together, this unspoken understanding between employers and employees formed the implicit "social contract" of the work relationship (Kochan & Shulman, 2007).

This relationship often caused employees to feel like children—the company was the "parent" (e.g., giving direction as well as an allowance, while also providing security) and the employee was the "dutiful child" (e.g., following orders and not questioning authority in exchange for the protections and benefits offered by the organization). Though employees were often frustrated with the repetition of their jobs and the autocratic nature of their supervisors, these corporate promises were generally enough for most people to justify the trade-offs.

The essential nature of this parent-child relationship remains in place at most organizations even today. While some companies have worked hard to develop cultures where employees are treated very well, others follow a more ruthless and domineering approach. Just like the actual parent-child relationship which exists at home, unless laws are directly and egregiously broken, there are no binding rules of behavior which require leaders to be kind to employees, or even civil.

This relationship developed as a result of the focus by organizations on efficiency. In large-scale operations, it was generally less expensive to purchase labor in bulk than to hire craftsmen by the hour to perform each task. For workers, this meant selling control over their time, energy, and talents to someone else. For corporations, the problem was utilization. Paying for 40 hours of labor if only 30 were needed was wasteful. The common understanding was (and still is) that all *means of production*—both human and technical—should be utilized to their fullest extent. The machines were less complex; they only had to be fueled and maintained. The humans, however, had to be *managed*; someone had to divide and coordinate the work, and to watch over the employees in order to make sure that they were productive and efficient.

Labor unions were created to protect the rights of workers. As jobs were progressively automated, more educated workers were needed to meet the requirements of higher-skilled roles. Largely due to legislation, working conditions improved in terms

of safety and health. While the legal definitions and fundamental nature of corporations remained intact and unchanged, the nature of the employment relationship did
not (Greider, 2003). It is no stretch to conclude that the "social contract" and the trust
it engendered between employees and their organizations has been irretrievably broken (Kochan & Shulman, 2007).

While the "parent-child" analogy remains true, the current employment relationship can also be described as that of "master-servant" given the imbalance of power
and distinct hierarchies that exist in most organizations (Greider, 2003). Employees
working for an organization are governed by different rights, privileges and legal protections than the general public. In essence, employees lose their "personhood" when
they go to work.

As Levering (1988, p. 62) observed:

> We generally accept as a given the contrast between our time at work and the rest of our lives.
> Once you enter the office or factory, you lose many of the rights you enjoy as a citizen. There's
> no process for challenging—or changing—bad decisions made by the authorities. There's no
> mechanism to vote for people to represent you in decision-making bodies . . . We take for
> granted that such rights and protections don't apply to the workplace, partly because most of us
> have never seen examples to the contrary.

Greider (2003, p. 49) further confirmed this societal disconnect when he described the
reality of work in modern America:

> In pursuit of "earning a living" most Americans go to work for someone else and thereby accept
> the employer's right to command their behavior in intimate detail. At the factory gate or the
> front office, people implicitly forfeit claims to self-direction and are typically barred from partici-
> pating in the important decisions that govern their daily efforts. Most employees lose any voice
> in how the rewards of the enterprise are distributed, the surplus wealth their own work helped
> to create. Basic rights the founders said were inalienable—free speech and freedom of assembly,
> among others—are effectively suspended, consigned to the control of others. In some ways, the
> employee also surrenders essential elements of self.

The general legal status of employees in the United States reinforces the model of uni-
lateral management control. The predominant rule of "at will" employment—the
right of an employer to terminate an employee for any reason or for basically no reason at all—contributes significantly to this uneven power dynamic (Summers, 2000).

Perversely, a boss who screams or curses at a subordinate is deemed to be
exercising "management prerogative", while the subordinate who responds by yelling
back or even asking for an apology can be fired on the spot. In addition, employees
"can be fired for doing what's right—making a moral choice—and they frequently
are" (Greider, 2003, p. 78).

A growing body of researchers strenuously argue that when individuals enter the
workplace, they do not (and should not) abdicate their right to be treated fairly and
humanely. At a bare minimum, most would agree that employers should be required

to observe workplace norms for mutual respect and professionalism. As Hornstein (1996, p. 143) noted:

> No matter what the circumstances, bosses may not abuse others. They may not lie, restrict, or dictate employees' behavior outside the workplace, threaten harm, or protect themselves at the expense of those more vulnerable. Positions of greater power in organizations' hierarchy do not grant license to show favoritism, humiliate or behave as masters or gods.

For nearly four decades now, management experts, scholars, practitioners, and authors of popular business books have urged employers to treat their employees with respect and dignity. Recommendations to date have placed a heavy emphasis on the need for strong leadership, fair employment policies, comprehensive benefit programs, grievance processes, and frequent communication. In addition, organizations have been urged to emphasize ethics, integrity, and fair dealing in the conduct of their business. Despite vigorous efforts, though, progress toward these goals has been painfully slow.

Relentless Focus on Results—But Not How They are Attained

The focus on the "results at any cost" strategy embraced by American corporations seems to be one of the primary drivers which helps to create toxic leaders and toxic cultures. If everyone agrees that the consequences of toxic leadership are so bad, though, how is it that these leaders are able to achieve such high levels of organizational success? Why does it seem that there are often no consequences for their toxic behavior? The answer is easy. Simply put, they get results— at least in the short-term.

> *Everyone who worked for him knew it [that he was a toxic leader] but the people that he worked for had no idea. Nor were they interested in knowing. All they cared about was that he was performing. So, it's hard to want to stay in an organization like that that only cares about performance and not the manner of performance.*

"Getting the job done" and "not failing" are uniformly considered to be a sacrosanct duty among high-achieving leaders. Most employees cannot conceive of *not* delivering results due to the high stakes involved; as a result, their collective focus is typically aimed at making the toxic leader look good. When this occurs, the toxic leader not only is credited with getting results, but he also receives the related promotions and rewards. The inherent paradox is that his success is largely based on the great sense of duty and loyalty that his people feel to the organization—but not to him.

> *The part that was most difficult was knowing that if we succeed, if we work hard . . . if we work our knuckles to the bone, we will succeed and these guys [the toxic leaders] will benefit from it.*

In my experience (and likely yours too), most leaders are typically intense and highly driven individuals. Though they are often very effective, their forceful personalities and passion to reach their targeted goals can cause great distress to employees. Organizations with a culture focused on "results at any cost" create a situation where individuals with certain types of personalities seem to thrive.

Due to their social competence and political skills, some high-performance leaders are also able to strategically abuse co-workers and yet continue to be evaluated positively by their supervisor (Yamada, 2008). They have been described as "abrasive personalities" (Levinson, 1978) and "expansive executives" (Kaplan, 1991), "great intimidators" (Kramer, 2006), "alpha risks" (Ludeman & Erlandson, 2006), and "tough bosses" (Daniel, 2009). Regardless of the label we ultimately elect to use, these individuals tend to suffer from a lack of awareness of their impact on others, and clearly wreak havoc in the workplace.

The actions of toxic leaders go beyond what is actually functional for the organization when there are signs of pain, injury, or distress being inflicted on another person. This begs the question: why would these leaders continue to engage in such negative behavior?

One hypothesis suggests that leaders who exhibit highly aggressive characteristics are narcissistic (self-obsessed), sociopathic (lacking social conscience), or even psychopathic (lacking basic empathy) (Schouten & Silver, 2012; Boddy, 2011; Babiak & Hare, 2006; Hare, 1993). The term "evil personality" has also been used to explain why some individuals use their power "to destroy the spiritual growth of others for the purpose of defending and preserving the integrity of their own sick selves" (Peck, 1998).

Similarly, others point to the personal deficiency of the leader and argues that they are, in fact, disturbed individuals who are power-hungry, enjoy hurting innocent people, or lack normal inhibitions and empathy (Schouten & Silver, 2012; Lubit, 2004). Still others suggest that these toxic behaviors have little to do with general work-related stress but are a result of an abuse of power that is "knowing and deliberate" (Horn, 2002; Hornstein, 1996).

Others focus less on individual deficiencies and explain that the behavior is due mostly to lack of awareness. These researchers argue that many people simply do not see the distress they are causing and are generally receptive to a different way of managing after they undergo coaching that draws attention to the problems that they are causing others or counseling (Crawshaw, 2007; Levinson, 1978). Ultimately, though, it is undisputed that something drives aggression in these individuals beyond the point of generally acceptable social norms.

The success of the "results at all costs" strategy was recently confirmed by a study in which researchers determined that aggressive leaders who are abusive to others are more likely to enjoy professional success than even their more competent rivals (Cheng, Tracy, Foulsham, Kingstone, & Henrick, 2013). Why? Because people are impressed by their dominance.

While not universally liked, the most dominant individuals were *feared* which led to an increase in their social standing and resulting organizational success. This two-part study looked at how "dominance" (defined as the use of force and intimidation to induce fear) and "prestige" (defined in the study as the appearance of skill and competency) can be used to achieve social rank and influence.

The researchers found that those rated as more dominant and prestigious were also rated as more influential. Ironically, while participants preferred leaders with prestige, they were actually more likely to choose dominant leaders. They also tended to be more forgiving of their bad behavior.

These results might help to explain the prevalence and high rate of success among aggressive leaders in business. As Furnham aptly noted (2009, p. 212):

> The business world often calls for (and rewards) arrogant, self-confident, and self-important people. But, as anyone who works with and for them knows, they can destabilize and destroy working groups by their deeply inconsiderate behavior.

Through a relentless focus on results at any cost and no consequences for the use of overly aggressive tactics to achieve them, our corporations are actually encouraging bad behavior that creates organizational toxicity for employees. This realistic perspective was offered by a somewhat pessimistic author who wryly noted (Ford, 2005, p. 138):

> In the real world, bullies are often the winners. They are the so-called tough bosses who have pushed their way to the top over the heads of their weaker and less aggressive colleagues. They are an archetype. They are the bulldogs, the pit bulls, the take-charge guys. They are the Donald Trump's of our lives.
>
> In the business world, bullies are rewarded. They are lionized. They are imitated and toadied to. Too often, the men and women who report to them adopt the same attitude toward the people they supervise, and so it goes down the line until you have a toxic work environment. Little wonder schools are incapable of routing bullies; the world around them can't and won't.

There seems to be a disconnect about what companies claim to want from leaders and the types of behavior they actually recognize and reward. What tends to be perceived as simply "strong management" in a corporate setting would normally be confrontational and out-of-line outside of the workplace. This type of behavior is rewarded because management turns a blind eye to the process—the *way*—by which the results are actually achieved.

While there is consensus that the behavior of abusive leaders is unacceptable, for some reason they continue to command our interest and attention. There is something about the phenomenon that is either so provocative or so repulsive (or maybe both), that we sometimes inadvertently seem to support it by our failure to intervene (Ford, 2005). Some have referred to this fascination with those who operate outside the rules as the "charisma of villainy" (Di Salvo, 2012).

Regardless of the reasons, though, people who work outside of the accepted norms attract and hold our interest—at either extreme (Nunberg, 2012). One can be both a genius and a jerk (think Steve Jobs, founder of Apple) or just a jerk. These outliers do not follow the accepted corporate rules and accepted norms; instead, they strategically use them to suit their own personal purposes and usually for their own personal gain (Rogers, 2011).

Psychological research over the past few years has suggested that there is an adaptive advantage created by overconfidence at work, but the trait often leads to errors. Inexplicably, even if that overconfidence produces sub-par results, others still perceive it positively. In other words, overconfident people are perceived as having more social status, and social status in the corporate world is golden (Belmi, Neale, Rieff, & Ulfe, 2020; Anderson, Brion, Moore, & Kennedy, 2012).

Another study highlights a similar result, but this time with respect to rudeness. Being rude is a categorically negative behavior by most standards; however, research suggests that we also see it as a sign of power. The ruder someone acts, the more convinced observers become that he or she is powerful, and therefore does not have to respect normal rules (Van Kleef, Homan, Finkenauer, Gundemir, & Stamkon, 2001).

Powerful people smile less, interrupt others more, and speak in a louder voice. When people do not respect the basic rules of social behavior, they lead others to believe that they have power, even if the observers would otherwise judge those violations as rude or flatly wrong (Treadway, Shaughnessy, Breland, Yang, & Reeves, 2013).

The net result of this prolonged focus on profit maximization has been to destabilize the psychological foundations of the corporations upon which the global economy relies. The economists were wrong. As brilliantly noted by Tim Richards (2012), referring to the chilling psychopath in the psychological horror film, *The Silence of the Lambs* (Wikipedia, n.d.):

> What you get when you have a human who is perfectly rational and utterly self-interested isn't an ideal economic specimen of the species. No, it's Hannibal Lecter in a business suit.

References

Anderson, C., Brion, S., Moore, D., & Kennedy, J. (2012, October). A status–enhancement account of overconfidence. *Journal of Personality and Social Psychology, 103*(4), 718–735.

Babiak, P., & Hare, R.D. (2006). *Snakes in suits*. New York: Harper Collins.

Belmi, P., Neale, M.A., Rieff, D. & R. Ulfe (2020). The social advantage of miscalibrated individuals: The relationship between social class and overconfidence and Its implications for class-based inequality. *Journal of Personality & Social Psychology. 118*(2), 254–282.

Boddy, C.R. (2011). *Corporate psychopaths: Organisational destroyers*. Palgrave Macmillan.

Cheng, J.T., Tracy, J.L., Foulsham, T., Kingstone, A., & Henrick, J. (2013). Two ways to the top: Evidence that dominance and prestige are distinct yet viable avenues to social rank and influence. *Journal of Personality & Social Psychology, 104*(1), 103–125.

Crawshaw, L. (2007). *Taming the abrasive manager*. Jossey-Bass; Levinson, H. (1978, May–June). The abrasive personality. *Harvard Business Review*, 86–94.

Daniel, T.A. (2009). *"Tough boss" or workplace bully: A grounded theory study of insights from human resource professionals*. Doctoral Dissertation, Fielding Graduate University. http://gradworks.umi.com/33/50/3350585.html.

DiSalvo, D. (2012). Why jerks get ahead. *Forbes*. http://www.forbes.com/sites/daviddisalvo/2012/08/18/why-jerks-get-ahead/.

Edwards, D. (1996). *Burning all illusions: A guide to personal and political freedom*. South End Press, p. 163.

Ford, C. (2005). *Against the grain: An irreverent view of Alberta*. McLelland & Stewart Ltd. at p 138.

Friedman, M. (1970, September 13). The social responsibility of business is to increase its profits. *The New York Times Magazine*. http://www.colorado.edu/studentgroups/libertarians/issues/friedman-soc-resp–business.html.

Furnham, A. (2009). Narcissism at work: The narcissistic personality and organizational relationships. In R. Morrison & S. Wright (Eds.), *Friends and enemies in organizations: A work psychology perspective* (pp. 168–194). Palgrave Macmillan.

Greider, W. (2009, May 6). *The future of the American dream*. The Nation. http://www.thenation.com/article/future-american-dream.

Greider, W. (2003). *The soul of capitalism: Opening paths to a moral economy*. Simon & Schuster.

Hare, R.D. (1993). *Without conscience: The disturbing world of psychopaths among us*. The Guilford Press.

Horn, S. (2002). *Take the bully by the horns: Stop unethical, uncooperative, or unpleasant people from running and ruining your life*. St. Martin's Griffin.

Hornstein, H.A. (1996). *Brutal bosses and their prey: How to identify and overcome abuse in the workplac*e. Riverhead Books.

Kaplan, R. (1991). *Beyond ambition*. Jossey-Bass Management Series.

Kochan, T. & Shulman, B. (2007, February 22). *A new social contract: Restoring dignity and balance to the economy*. Briefing Paper #184. www.epi.org.

Kramer, R.M. (2006). The great intimidators. *Harvard Business Review*. http://hbr.org/2006/02/the-great-intimidators/ar/1.

Levering, R. (1988). *A great place to work: What makes some employers so good-and most so bad*. Random House, p. 62.

Levinson, H. (1978, May–June). The abrasive personality. *Harvard Business Review*, 86–94.

Lubit, R. (2004). *Coping with toxic managers, subordinates . . . and other difficult people*. Financial Times Press.

Ludeman, K., & Erlandson, E. (2006). *Alpha male syndrome*. Harvard Business School Press.

Makower, J. (2006, November 24). *Milton Friedman and the social responsibility of business*. http://www.greenbiz.com/news/2006/11/24/milton-friedman-and-social-responsibility-business. p. 31.

Nunberg, G. (2012, August 15). *Why do we idolize jerks?* http://www.alternet.org/culture/why-do-we-idolize-jerks.

Peck, M.S. (1998). *People of the lie: The hope for healing human evil*. Touchtone.

Richards, T. (2012, May 10). Is your CEO a psychopath? *The Psy-Fi Blog*. http://www.psyfitec.com/2012/05/is-your-ceo-psychopath.html.

Rogers, K. (2011, November 3). *Why being the office jerk could pay off*. Fox Business. http://www.foxbusiness.com/personal-finance/2011/11/03/workplace-jerks-make-more–money/#ixzz2NMghSBqR.

Schouten, R. & Silver, J. (2012). *Almost a psychopath: Do I (or does someone I know) have a problem with manipulation and lack of empathy?* Hazelden.

Summers, C.W. (2000). Employment at will in the United States: The divine right of employers. *University of Pennsylvania Journal of Labor & Employment Law*, 3(65), 67–68.

Treadway, D.C., Shaughnessy, B.A., Breland, J.W., Yang, J. & Reeves, M. (2013). Political skill and the job performance of bullies. *Journal of Managerial Psychology*, 28(3), 273–289.

VanKleef, M. Homan, G.A., Finkenauer, A.C., Gundemir, S., & Stamkon, E. (2011). Breaking the rules to rise to power: How norm violators gain power in the eyes of others. *Social Psychological and Personality Science, 2*(5), 500–507.

Wikipedia (n.d.). *Silence of the lambs.* https://en.wikipedia.org/wiki/The_Silence_of_the_Lambs_(film).

Yamada, D.C. (2008). Workplace bullying and ethical leadership. *Journal of Values-Based Leadership, 1*(2). http://papers.ssrn.com/sol3/papers.cfm?abstractid=1301554.

_____

Leadership Changes Everything: Types of Leaders and How They Impact Employees and Their Organizations

Chapter 3
Toxic Leaders vs. "Tough" Bosses: Who They Are, What They Do, and Why They Are Tolerated and/or Rewarded

As a scholar-practitioner working at the intersection of leadership, ethics, and human resources, the paradox of how otherwise smart and talented people can so easily turn into toxic and unethical leaders has consumed much of my research agenda. I have conducted research studies in the corporate sector (focused on the perspectives of corporate HR practitioners and executives) and in a military environment (with officers attending the U.S. Army Command and General Staff College in Fort Leavenworth, Kansas and also officers stationed at the Fort Knox, Kentucky base).

This chapter draws heavily from those prior studies, a comprehensive review of the academic and military leadership on topic, and from other work in which I have been involved over the course of many years in the field. Let's dive in and explore who they are, what they actually do, why they do it, and why anyone—most importantly you—should care?

General

The word "toxic" is defined as being *poisonous*, or *extremely harsh, malicious*, or *harmful* (*Merriam-Webster Online Dictionary*, n.d.). The term became associated with leadership when Marcia Whicker (1996) first coined the term "toxic leadership" in 1996 as a way to describe a highly destructive leadership style that we will closely examine throughout this book.

Toxic Leaders—Who They Are and What They Do

Whether they are labeled as *toxic leaders* (the typical term used in a military context) or *workplace bullies* (the common label used in a corporate environment), these individuals are highly destructive (Lipman-Blumen, 2005; Whicker, 1996; Kellerman, 2004; Steele, 2011). They act aggressively toward their subordinates, are highly critical and dismissive, demand almost blind loyalty, frequently blame or take credit for the work of others, and they play mind games strategically designed to keep people off balance.

They exert their dominance and exploit their power and authority by threatening, intimidating, yelling, or engaging in vicious and explosive verbal assaults intended to demean, undermine, and publicly humiliate those on the receiving end.

https://doi.org/10.1515/9783111201771-003

Though rare, they sometimes engage in physical attacks too. Their subordinates generally hate or fear them (often both), and usually work very hard to stay out of their line of sight.

Whicker (1996, p. 11) describes toxic leaders as: ". . . maladjusted, malcontent, and often malevolent, even malicious. They succeed by tearing others down. They glory in turf protection, fighting and controlling rather than uplifting followers."

While using the term "bad leadership" to describe the behaviors often deemed by others to be "toxic", Kellerman (2004) proposes a typology that includes seven groups of behaviors: "incompetent, rigid, intemperate, callous, corrupt, insular, and evil" (p. 38). She suggests that the first three types of bad leadership are bad as in *ineffective*, while the remaining groups are bad as in *unethical* (p. 39). Kellerman further suggests that a leader who has an excessive need for power is likely toxic and that "in its more extreme form, a craving for power can be dangerous" (p. 20).

Lipman-Blumen (2005, pp. 4–5) suggests that leaders are toxic:

> when they inflict serious and enduring harm on their followers by using influence tactics that are extremely harsh and/or malicious. In short, toxic leaders exhibit destructive behaviors that work to decay their followers' morale, motivation, and self-esteem.

She reports that toxic leaders utilize a range of destructive behaviors from undermining, demeaning, marginalizing, intimidating, demoralizing, and disenfranchising followers, to "incapacitating, imprisoning, terrorizing, torturing, or killing others, including members of their entourage" (p. 19). She further explains:

> To count as toxic, these behaviors and qualities of character must inflict some reasonably serious and enduring harm on their followers and their organizations. The intent to harm others or to enhance the self at the expense of others distinguishes seriously toxic leaders from the careless or unintentional toxic leaders (p. 18).

Sutton (2007) suggests that two key elements must be considered in the determination of whether an individual is "toxic": (1) after talking with the individual, does the "target" feel oppressed, humiliated, de-energized or belittled by the person? and (2) does the alleged negative leader aim his venom at people who are *less* powerful rather than at those who are *more* powerful? (p. 9). The first element assesses the effect of the leader on others, while the second element reflects Sutton's "kiss up and kick down" concept. By this, he means that a negative leader will work hard to make a positive impression on his superior regardless of the downstream impact on his people (p. 9).

Pelletier (2010) identifies several dimensions of leader toxicity. These include leader breakdown of subordinate self-esteem, threats to job and/or personal security, promoting a culture of inequity, intimidating employees both physically and mentally, and a lack of honesty.

Other persistent behaviors of a toxic leader include, among others: avoiding subordinates, behaving aggressively toward others, blaming others for their own problems, being overly critical of work that is done well, and intimidating and humiliating others (Ashforth, 1994; Kellerman, 2004; Lipman-Blumen, 2005).

Use of Power—Personalized vs. Socialized

At its core, leadership is about power and the influence which leaders use to get things done. While there are numerous types of power, our interest focuses on the theory espoused by McClelland (1975). He suggests that there are two primary forms of power: *personalized* power—that is, power used for advancing personal gain and influence, and *socialized* power—when the leader's power is used for the benefit of others.

With *personalized* power, the view is selfish and a leader typically achieves short-term results based on their own self-interest. Common behaviors include being rude and overbearing, exploitative, dominant, risk, defensive, impulsive, and erratic. It is not a far stretch to presume that a personalized power orientation might drive people toward occupations promoting aggressive strategy and forceful action—like the military.

With *socialized* power, the leader's view is primarily focused on others, is longer-term in focus, and empowers others to achieve collective goals. Common behaviors include collaboration, proactive development of people, and being a source of strength to people and the organization which he serves. These two forms of power are not mutually exclusive. It is possible for a leader to use his power to benefit others but, at the same time, he can also gain personally. The real distinction is that when personalized power dominates, the leader gains—most often at the expense and to the detriment of their subordinates.

Toxic leaders appear to be characterized by a *personalized* power orientation given their general need for control and their excessive self-interest (Padilla, Hogan, & Kaiser, 2007). They are willing to work long hours to gain support and to achieve their goals—at the expense of the organization and their subordinates. In the extreme, toxic leaders can become "intoxicated" by power and even engage in wrongdoing simply because they *can*—and because they feel confident that they can get away with it.

Senior leaders have many temptations due to their privileged access and decreasing checks and balances as they move up within the organization. As a result, highly intelligent people can be seduced into taking more risks and making poor decisions as their ego becomes ever more inflated due to their escalating success within the organization. This combination of factors can lead to an individual's sense of entitlement that they are "special" and exempt from the rules that they apply to others (Daniel, 2013). We will more closely examine these ethical risks in a later chapter.

Along similar lines, there is support for the idea that the acquisition and successful use of power tends to corrupt the power holder in several respects: (1) power becomes an end in itself; (2) the power holder develops an inflated sense of self-worth; (3) power is used increasingly for personal, rather than organizational purposes; and (4) the power holder de-values the worth of others (Kipnis, Castell, Gergen, & Mauch, 1976). In addition, they may attribute the successes of their subordinates to themselves.

Distinctions Between Toxic Leaders in a Military vs. Corporate Context

There are some interesting distinctions between destructive leaders who operate in a military context and those operating in the corporate business world. These differences will be explored next.

The Toxic Military Leader: "It's All About Me"

According to a significant internal survey by the U.S. Army, an estimated 20% of American soldiers report that they have suffered under a toxic leader (Ulmer, 2012). So, what does it mean to the military for an officer to be "toxic"?

The term is generally applied to a leader who "appears driven by self-centered careerism at the expense of their subordinates and unit, and whose style is characterized by abusive and dictatorial behavior that promotes an unhealthy organizational climate" (Reed, 2004). Similarly, others have characterized toxic leadership as "an apparent lack of concern for the well-being of subordinates", "a personality or interpersonal technique that negatively affects organizational climate", and "a conviction by subordinates that the leader is motivated primarily by self-interest" (Dobbs & Do, 2018).

Supported by a strong culture that considers mission accomplishment to be almost sacrosanct, toxic military leaders are intensely mission-focused which is, of course, entirely appropriate in that environment. It becomes a double-edged sword, though, when they fail to consider *how* their results are actually attained. They tend to adopt a "results at any cost" strategy that does not factor in how working a rigorous and demanding work schedule (often including weekends) affects soldiers and their families.

The impact on people is similarly harsh when a toxic leader ambitiously over-extends the unit on projects undertaken solely to enhance their own standing in the eyes of their commander. In these situations, soldiers are often required to work for extended periods of time without adequate personnel or equipment on the chance that the toxic leader will get some extra benefit from his superiors by taking on the assignment. Consequently, the subordinates of toxic leaders often feel that toxic leaders have no empathy for and simply do not care about them, creating high levels of organizational cynicism (Ulmer, 2012, p. 48). The result is that they either burn out and leave due to the relentless demands and harsh treatment or, perhaps worse yet, stay but feel angry and demoralized—not exactly the conditions to inspire or build a cohesive work unit.

Toxic leaders are results-driven to a fault, while wholeheartedly embracing a "kiss up and kick down" style of operating. Their advanced interpersonal skills allow them to schmooze and get along well with senior leaders at the top echelon. This political savvy, coupled with their accomplishment of near-impossible missions, causes their superiors to hold them with high regard. Their solid reputation for being bright, personable, technically competent, and for getting things done overwhelms any suspicion by their boss that their means might not justify the ends (Daniel & Metcalf, 2015):

> That's kind of how those people work. Everybody at their level or higher just thinks they're a charming, hard working person. Then people underneath them just think they're the devil and wonder: "what do they see in him? Why do they like him? Why do they promote him and give him good evaluations?" He's horrible but that's their [the toxic leader's] modus operandi. I think they kick butt and they work their people hard and then take the credit for it.

While toxic leaders are often revered by their superiors, their subordinates know all too well how abusive and excessively self-interested they can be. They are widely viewed as having little regard for people other than themselves. They are also perceived as being laser-focused on securing their next promotion or on the next opportunity to impress their superiors (but not necessarily on doing what is right for their subordinates or in the U.S. Army's long-term best interest). In fact, they sometimes get involved in activities *only* if they believe that a senior leader will be available for them to impress.

This self-absorption causes subordinates to see the motive of their leader as being less about ensuring the Army's success, and more along the lines of *"it's all about me, me . . . and me"*. Not surprisingly, toxic leaders do not tend to see themselves as arrogant, self-interested, destructive, or cruel. If they are aware at all of their impact on others, they rationalize their behavior as being *"tough"* and *"mission driven"* while denigrating those who object to their operating style by calling them *"whiners"* and *"crybabies"*.

The truth is that their behavior is both tough and mission driven; however, it goes far beyond that—their interactions with subordinates are widely perceived as harsh, abusive, intimidating, threatening, humiliating, and almost always demoralizing to those who work for them. They do not seem to care about the impact of their actions on their people as long as the mission is accomplished. The result is an excessive number of transfer requests or full resignations from the Army by soldiers under their command.

Developing and retaining talented subordinates is critical to the success of an all-volunteer Army like we have in the U.S. The failure of a toxic leader to coach and inspire others may be their most lasting and destructive impact on the organization. Think about it: when a person works for a corporation, they can quit and go to work for another company but stay in their profession. However, when military personnel find their leaders to be so intolerable that they would prefer to leave the service, all they can do is resign and leave the military profession altogether, along with their pension.

Dave Matsuda (2014) offered a disturbing synopsis of the problem as it occurs within a military context: "Outside the wire, the enemy is the enemy; inside the wire, the command climate is the enemy."

By the time the damage they have caused to their unit is well understood, the toxic leader is long gone, happily promoted and relocated to their next assignment—where they start the destructive cycle all over again.

The Toxic Corporate Leader: "I'm Gonna Get You—Whatever It Takes"

The U.S. Army most assuredly is not the only large organization with a toxic leader problem—the corporate sector also has its fair share of destructive leaders. In that arena, however, they are generally referred to as *workplace bullies.*

In a 2021 U.S. national survey on the phenomenon, about 30% of adult Americans reported that they have directly experienced bullying at work (defined in the survey as "repeated mistreatment: abusive conduct that is threatening, intimidating, humiliating, work sabotage, or work abuse") while another 19% report that they have witnessed it occurring at work—which translates to 79.3 million employed Americans who are affected by workplace bullying (Workplace Bullying Institute, 2021).

Like toxic leaders, corporate bullies frequently misuse their power and authority, are excessively self-focused, prone to emotional outbursts, and often treat people unfairly (Daniel & Metcalf, 2015). But there is one key difference: unlike the toxic military leader whose actions tend to negatively affect the command climate of the entire unit, toxic corporate types tend to single out a single employee to torment, humiliate, or intimidate for a period of time—until they move on to their next target.

Their motive is described as *"I'm gonna get you—whatever it takes".* Some targets describe the experience as being *"an all-out personal attack"* (Daniel & Metcalf, 2015). Indeed, one of my earliest studies supported these sentiments by finding that toxic corporate leaders act with *malice*—defined as *"the desire to cause pain, injury, or distress to another"* (Daniel, 2009; *Merriam-Webster Dictionary*, n.d.).

What this means is that their behavior is intentionally abusive and purposefully targeted toward specific individuals, usually with the intent to drive the person out of the organization. Bottom line: the individual is well aware of what they are doing and continues to do it anyway, regardless of the damage or pain they cause.

Characteristics of a "Tough Boss"

Tough Bosses Everywhere: "Tough but Fair"

Although there are some differences between toxic leaders based on whether they are operating in a military or corporate context, studies have shown that tough bosses are virtually the same in both environments. Think of tough bosses as almost the polar opposite of toxic leaders. While toxic leaders are almost universally bad for an organization, tough bosses—people who both get things done and care for their people—are absolutely essential for success.

The profile of a tough boss most often looks like this: they are professional, self-controlled, highly self-aware, emotionally mature, results-oriented, and strive to make long-term decisions that are good for both their people and the organization (Daniel, 2009; Daniel & Metcalf, 2015). Like toxic leaders, tough bosses are also passionate about getting results; in fact, they are sometimes perceived as nearly *maniacal* in their efforts to meet their goals.

As a result, they are by no means "soft" or easy to work for. A key differentiator, though, is that tough bosses make sure to show that they really care about their people—by taking time to mentor and coach, by getting to know their people on a personal level, through frequent two-way communications, by recognizing and celebrating performance, by taking personal responsibility for mistakes in their department, and by acting quickly to resolve interpersonal conflicts or address other work-related concerns. This more humane approach results in a generally positive work climate (at least most days). People who work for tough bosses consistently characterize them as *"tough but fair"*—and generally feel a great deal of loyalty and respect for them.

Lest the picture seem too rosy, though, the challenge of working for a tough boss should not be minimized. They are usually intense and highly-driven individuals. Their demanding (and sometimes perfectionistic) expectations create a fair amount of tension and stress for those who work for them. The difference is that employees understand that their drive for results is not personal or mean-spirited; instead, they understand that the adherence to high standards is meant to benefit both them and the organization.

It is important to note that tough bosses place a heavy emphasis on employee development and spend a great deal of time mentoring and coaching their subordinates. This focus, coupled with their adherence to high standards, helps to ensure that their organizations are continuously building a pipeline of strong, well-trained future leaders. Ultimately, this may be their greatest legacy to the long-term success and sustainability of their organizations.

While it should come as no surprise, employees who work for them are usually adamant that tough bosses should not be admonished or cautioned to "tone it down" simply because they set the bar high. In fact, they pretty uniformly suggest that these tough and results-oriented leaders are absolutely *essential* for organizational success —and I could not agree with them more (Daniel & Metcalf, 2015).

Consequences of Toxic Leadership at the Top

It should now be clear that toxic leaders can (and often do) achieve extraordinary results, but the price is often sky high given their destructive impact on people in the organization; however, they just don't seem to care. They just want to get the job done as fast as humanly possible so that they can secure their next promotion and move on up. As a result of their short-term, "take no prisoners" focus, they invariably leave their organizations in far worse shape than when they started.

Outcomes range from mutiny and death (in a military context) to an erosion of trust, increased turnover, domestic violence, higher absenteeism, increased alcohol and drug use, burnout, depression, as well as reductions in employee health, motivation, productivity, happiness, and reduced job satisfaction.

As if all that were not enough, the organization is also often hit with related costs arising from increases in workers' compensation claims, plus marked spikes in both mental health and medical expenses (predominantly due to increased stress) incurred by the target and sometimes also members of their family too. In combination, these predictable outcomes seem like more than enough reason to want to do something about these destructive leaders.

Understanding Your Own Toxic Tendencies

Assessing Toxic Leader Behaviors

Some of you are by now probably thinking to yourself: *Is my boss a toxic leader?* Or, hitting a little closer to home, you might be asking yourself: *What about me—am I toxic or just tough?* To get a handle on either answer, here are the most common behaviors associated with toxic leaders. Check "yes" to any and all that seem to apply.

Do you (or someone you know):

Toxic Leader Behaviors

1. Care about achieving results so much that you fail to consider the impact of the work and schedule on employees and their families?
2. Excessively focus on your own pay and promotions?
3. Take credit for the work of others?
4. Always think you are right and that your ideas are the best ones?

5. Fail to get to know your employees on a personal level?
6. Unconcerned about or oblivious to employee morale?
7. Fail to allow discussion or debate because you consider it a threat to your authority?
8. Often make short-term decisions that make you look good but that are likely to be detrimental to the organization in the long run?
9. Appear charming and personable to your boss but treat your employees badly?
10. Engage in angry tirades and/or attack people verbally or physically?
11. Intentionally seek to threaten, intimidate, or humiliate people?
12. Treat people unfairly, inconsistently, and with a lack of respect?
13. Blame others for mistakes but take no personal responsibility?
14. Have an inflated sense of self-importance?
15. Commit to meeting goals without securing the proper funding, resources, or personnel?
16. Fail to mentor or develop your employees?
17. Create a climate of fear, anxiety, or mistrust at work?

Getting a Handle on Your Own Toxic Tendencies

It is sometimes easy to identify someone else as a toxic leader, but harder to be objective when assessing your own behaviors. As a result, it is a good idea to invite other people to weigh in. This requires being vulnerable and asking for direct and candid opinions about your effect on others. You will get the most benefit from talking with colleagues and friends who you know will be brutally frank with you (although it will undoubtedly be hard to hear).

Get an executive coach who can help you critically examine yourself and who can also provide you with strategies and tools to support you as you adjust your way of operating at work. Take time to listen and pay closer attention to your impact on others. If you have not yet explored the Myers-Briggs Type Inventory (MBTI®), consider taking this assessment (or something similar) to learn more about your preferences and personality style (Myers-Briggs Type Indicator, n.d.). Participate in your company's system of 360-degree feedback assessment to see how you are coming across to your boss, peers, and subordinates at work.

Work on improving your self-awareness, self-regulation, motivation, empathy, and social skills—all of which make up your emotional intelligence. The data showing that emotional intelligence is a key differentiator between star performers and others is irrefutable [26]. Above all, though, refrain from making excuses to yourself or others about your use of power and authority in ways that are motivated, at least in part, by ego and self-interest. After all, these are *your* negative behaviors—own them. And then, most importantly, take action to fix them.

Any change is tough, but until you decide that changing yourself is absolutely required and you begin the hard work that it will take to get there, leading with a toxic twist will remain your default *modus operandi*—and history suggests that it will ultimately derail your career.

Understanding Your Own Tough Boss Behaviors

Assessing Tough Boss Behaviors

Now that you have some idea about toxic tendencies, here are the most common tough boss behaviors uncovered in our studies and review of the relevant literature. Check "yes" to any and all that seem to apply. Do you (or someone you know):

Tough Boss Behaviors

1. Care about achieving results but also consider the impact of the work and schedule on your employees and their families?
2. Have tough and demanding expectations for yourself and your subordinates about achieving results?
3. Have a high level of self-awareness, empathy, and emotional maturity?
4. Show care and concern for your people?
5. Act professionally and with self-control at work?
6. Seek to resolve conflicts fairly and quickly?
7. Give credit and recognition to others?
8. Celebrate and reward the successful efforts of your subordinates?
9. Treat people fairly, consistently, and with respect?
10. Take time to mentor, coach, and develop your subordinates?
11. Take personal responsibility for mistakes in your unit or department?
12. Make decisions that are in the long-term best interest of the organization?
13. Seek to develop a positive and respectful work climate?

If you determine that you have a significant number of these attributes, kudos to you for exhibiting the type of leadership that creates a positive and respectful work environment –one that is associated with long-term positive outcomes both for employees, as well as for your organization. Although employees may feel pushed and challenged (as noted earlier, it is not necessarily easy for an employee to work for a tough boss), they are also likely to be highly productive, feel that they are being mentored and are expanding their skills, while also feeling respected and appreciated at work.

The "So What?"

In summary, the evidence is unequivocal that toxic leaders are bad for business. Conversely, working for a caring, empathetic, and supportive boss—even one with demanding expectations—has direct and cost-saving health outcomes for employees, as well as important organizational benefits related to higher employee engagement, job satisfaction, and reduced counterproductive behavior (Nowak & Zak, 2019).

Hopefully these checklists have provided a quick way for you to assess your own behaviors (or those of your boss, and maybe both). Why is this important? Armed with this knowledge, you can decide to proactively change some of your own less-than-desirable behaviors or you can proactively help a leader with toxic tendencies become more self-aware so that they can work to improve their own behavior.

For organizations, clearer distinctions between toxic leaders and tough bosses can help with quicker identification of both. This means that tough bosses can be more quickly recognized and rewarded for their constructive leadership style, and toxic leaders can be paired with a coach or mentor to try to get an early handle on their destructive tendencies.

References

Ashforth, B.E. (1994). Petty tyranny in organizations. *Human Relations, 47*, 755–778.

Daniel, T.A. & Metcalf, G.S. (2015). *Crossing the line: An examination of toxic leadership in the U.S. Army.* doi: 10.13140/RG.2.1.2700.4969. https://www.academia.edu/11743522/Crossing_the_Line_An_Examination_of_Toxic_Leadership_in_the_U_S_Army.

Daniel, T.A. & Metcalf, G.S. (2015). Are you a toxic leader or just a tough boss? SHRM's *HR Magazine, 60*(6). https://www.shrm.org/hr-today/news/hr-magazine/pages/070815-toxic-leader-or-tough-boss.aspx.

Daniel, T.A. (2013, July). Executive success and the increased potential for ethical failure, *SHRM quarterly legal report.* http://www.shrm.org/LegalIssues/EmploymentLawAreas/Documents/Legal%20Report0713.pdf?homepage=marquee.

Daniel, T.A. (2009). *"Tough boss" or workplace bully: A grounded theory study of insights from human resource professionals.* Doctoral Dissertation. http://search.proquest.com/docview/305169091.

Daniel, T.A. (2012). Caught in the crossfire: When HR practitioners become targets of bullying. *Employment Relations Today, 39*(1), 9–16. http://onlinelibrary.wiley.com/doi/10.1002/ert.21349/abstract.

Dobbs, J.M. & Do, J.J. (2018, January 11). The impact of perceived toxic leadership on cynicism in officer candidates. *Armed Forces & Society.* http://journals.sagepub.com/doi/full/10.1177/0095327X17747204.

Kellerman, B. (2004). *Bad leadership: What it is, how it happens, why it matters.* Harvard Business School Press.

Kipnis, D., Castell, P.J., Gergen, P.J. & Mauch, D. (1976). Metamorphic effects of power. *Journal of Applied Psychology, 61*, 127–135.

Lipman-Blumen, J. (2005). *The allure of toxic leaders: Why we follow destructive bosses and corrupt politicians—and how we can survive them.* Oxford University Press.

Matsuda, D. (2014, May 24). *A study of Army suicides in Iraq in 2010–2014.* https://www.linkedin.com/pulse/20140524145604-76082895-a-study-of-army-suicides-in-iraq-a-2010-study-in-2014-context.

McClelland, D.C. (1975). *Power: The inner experience.* Irvington.

Merriam-Webster Dictionary (Online). *Definition of toxic.* https://www.merriam-webster.com/dictionary/toxic.

Merriam-Webster Dictionary (Online). *Definition of malice.* http://www.merriam-webster.com/dictionary/malice.

Myers-Briggs Type Indicator (n.d.). https://www.themyersbriggs.com/en-US/Products-and-Services/Myers-Briggs.

Nowak, K.M. & Zak, P. (2019). Empathy enhancing antidotes for interpersonally toxic leaders. *Consulting Psychology Journal: Practice and Research, 72*(2), 119–133.

Padilla, A. Hogan, R. & Kaiser, R.B. (2007). The toxic triangle: Destructive leaders, susceptible followers, and conducive environments, *Leadership Quarterly, 18*(3), 176–194.

Pelletier, K. L. (2010). Leader toxicity: An empirical investigation of toxic behavior and rhetoric. *Leadership, 6*(4) 373–389.

Reed, G.E. (2004). Toxic leaders. *Military Review*, 67–71. http://www.au.af.mil/au/awc/awcgate/milreview/reed.pdf.

Steele, J.P. (2011). *Technical Report 2011-3: Antecedents and consequences of toxic leadership in the U.S. Army: A two-year review and recommended solutions.* Center for Army Leadership. http://usacac.Army.mil/CAC2/Repository/CASAL_TechReport2011-3_ToxicLeadership.pdf.

Sutton, R.I. (2007). *The no asshole rule: Building a civilized workplace and surviving one that isn't.* Warner Business Books.

Ulmer, W.F. (2012, June). Toxic leadership. *Army*, 47–52 at 48.

Whicker, M.L. (1996). *Toxic leaders: When organizations go bad.* Quorum Books.

Workplace Bullying Institute (WBI) *2021 U.S. Workplace Bullying Study* (2021, February 23). https://workplacebullying.org/2021-wbi-survey/.

Chapter 4
Exceptional Leaders: Who They Are, What They Do, and Why They Are So Rare

We all know that bad leaders drive people away. Conversely, an organization populated with a healthy number of good leaders helps to improve employee retention and satisfaction, inspire and motivate the workforce, increase the overall well-being of employees, and contribute to making the organization a great place to work. So, if good leaders can do all of that, it prompts an empirical examination of this question: what is the impact of *great* ones?

In this chapter we will focus on what it is that makes a leader exceptional in the eyes of the people that they lead. In addition to a review of the available literature on the topic, this chapter is also informed by an empirical study with the U.S. Army which is foundational to this book. Further details of the findings of this study are summarized in *Appendix III*.

Review of the Relevant Literature

There are many ways to finish the sentence "Leadership is . . ." or "Great leaders are . . ." In fact, as Stogdill (1948) pointed out in his review of leadership research, there are almost as many definitions of leadership as there are authors who write about the topic. This has led Bennis and Nanus (1985) to the somewhat cynical observation:

> Never have so many labored so long to say so little. Multiple interpretations of leadership exist, each providing a sliver of insight but each remaining an incomplete and wholly inadequate explanation. (p. 4)

Similarly, in his path-breaking book, *Leadership*, James MacGregor Burns (1978) observed that "leadership is one of the most observed and least understood phenomena on earth". To my knowledge, there is still no universal consensus about how it should be defined even though scholars and practitioners have been studying the phenomenon for more than a century!

A review of the scholarly studies on leadership shows that there is a wide variety of different theoretical approaches to explain the complexities of the leadership process (Bass & Stogdill, 1990; Bryman, Collinson, Grint, Jackson, & Uhl-Bien, 2011; Bryman, 1992; Day & Antonakis, 2012; Gardner, 1990; Hickman, 2009; Mumford, 2006; Rost, 1991). Some researchers conceptualize leadership as a *trait* (Stogdill, 1948; Mann, 1959; Stogdill, 1974; Lord, DeVader & Alliger, 1986) or as *skills* (Mumford, Zaccaro, Harding, Jacobs, & Fleishman, 2000; Katz, 1955). Others characterize leadership as a *style*

https://doi.org/10.1515/9783111201771-004

or *behavior* (Hemphill & Coons, 1957; Cartwright & Zander, 1960; Blake & Mouton, 1964, 1985; Bowers & Seashore, 1966).

Still other researchers view leadership from a *relational standpoint* (Burns, 1978; Greenleaf, 1970). These are just a few examples of the voluminous theories used to explain the construct; an attempt to cover all of the suggested approaches would require writing a book (or several). Leadership has been studied using both qualitative and quantitative methods in many contexts, including small groups, military groups, and large-scale corporations, among others. Collectively, the research findings on leadership from all of these areas help to provide a rich picture of this complex process. Despite the significant amount of work that has been conducted so far, though, its complexity continues to present "a major challenge to practitioners and researchers interested in understanding the nature of leadership" (Northouse, 2013).

What Makes a Leader Exceptional?

Personal Excellence and the Achievement of High Standards

Both good leaders and exceptional leaders are distinguished by their use of these core practices which help to create a positive workplace climate while also achieving strong results:

> They *care about their people* (e.g., get to know them on a personal basis, are compassionate, supportive and approachable, and they pay attention to the impact of work on both the soldier and his family).

> They *develop their people* (e.g., mentors and coaches regularly, offers honest and constructive feedback, communicate openly and frequently, allow "freedom to maneuver", and provide both family and career counseling).

> Moreover, they *exhibit high levels of emotional intelligence* (e.g., they are empathetic, calm under pressure, they establish a climate of mutual trust and respect, they really listen, and they are highly self-aware of their impact on others).

> They are intensely *focused on mission accomplishment* (e.g., lead from the front, have high standards for self and others, and exhibit a "tough but fair" approach); and

> They *lead with tomorrow in mind* (e.g., make decisions that are in the long-term best interests of the organization).

Their consistent focus on both personal excellence and the achievement of high standards as evidenced by these observations:

You could tell that he actually cared about people and he didn't just pretend. He would ask personal questions and give you eye contact and listen to the answers and care about the answer. He had a reputation as being extremely competent, but he also had a reputation for really caring about his people—and leaders can't fake that.

They really led from the front. They really embodied everything they said they were going to do. They had a standard and they not only held themselves to that standard, but they also held their subordinates to the same standard.

The best guy I've ever worked for in my life. He's just amazing in every way. He cared about every person [who worked for him]. He worked well and everybody worked together as a team. It was just an amazing experience working for him . . . He was tough but he kept to his standards.

He was one of those leaders that took you out of your comfort zone, made you strive for excellence. If you tripped, he might give you a little bit of a spanking but it was not "you're terrible and I'm going to end your career"- type, it was "hey you've made a mistake and I'm going to help you improve yourself".

Care and Connect in a Highly Personalized Manner

The crucial differentiator between a *good* leader and a *great* one is that an exceptional leader can be distinguished by the **highly personalized caring** that they extend to both people and their families. This is consistent with the types of intense and close relationships with subordinates that "superbosses" nurture and develop (Finkelstein, 2016).

The relationships exceptional leaders establish with people they supervise goes well beyond just showing concern. They succeed in creating a positive workplace climate and accomplishing the organization's results by caring and connecting with their people in a deeply personal way (through mentoring, counseling, coaching, and frequent two-way communication). This deep sense of personal commitment and caring creates high levels of mutual trust and makes people feel genuinely valued and respected.

As evidenced by their frequent communication, mentoring, counseling, and efforts to develop the individual for future assignments, exceptional leaders exhibit a holistic personal concern about the people they supervise—not just as people there to do a job, but also as human beings with families, emotions, and real-life concerns and issues. Those who report to an exceptional leader unequivocally know and feel that the leader cares—*really cares*—about them on a personal level.

The significant amount of time invested by an exceptional leader mentoring, counseling, and developing their people results in a high level of mutual trust, inspiration, deep respect, open communication, and unwavering loyalty as these interview comments confirm:

I think the level of which they [great leaders] care and the way that they show it is what probably differentiates them most from everyone else. It builds loyalty right off the bat.

He was genuine.

I think they had there was a caring that they gave to us. Maybe [it] was that they cared what was going on in our lives outside of [work]. They were always in touch with us outside of work—making sure that we were doing okay with our families or our friends or what was going on. That really kind of touched us, I think.

A visual representation of the study's findings is in Figure 1:

Figure 1: Characteristics of Tough Bosses and Exceptional Leaders. Daniel, T.A. & Metcalf, G.S. (2015). *Crossing the line: An examination of toxic leadership in the U.S. Army.* doi: 10.13140/RG.2.1.2700.4969.

Figure 2 shows another visual representation of exceptional leaders as they compare to toxic leaders and tough bosses:

What We Learned:
Side-by-Side Comparison

Great Leader/Tough Boss	Toxic Leader
Cares about soldiers Gets to know soldiers on a personal basis Compassionate, supportive and approachable Pays attention to impact of work on soldier and family	**Cares about self** Actions undertaken so he can look good and "move up" Excessive self-interest/lack of concern for organization Works the system to his personal advantage
Develops soldiers Mentors and coaches soldiers Offers honest and constructive feedback Communicates openly and frequently Allows "freedom to maneuver" Provides family and career counseling	**Lack of concern for soldiers** Not interested in getting to know soldiers Does not engage in mentoring or coaching Transactional view of soldiers Malicious and abusive
High emotional intelligence Empathetic Calm under pressure Establishes climate of mutual trust and respect Listens to others Highly self-aware	**Low emotional intelligence** Incapable of expressing much empathy Frequent emotional outbursts Develops climate of fear Fails to listen to others Lack of self-awareness
Mission-focused results Leads from the front High standards for self and others "Tough but fair" in approach Long-term emphasis	**Mission-focused results** Gets results in order to get promoted/look good No regard for impact on people Abuse of power/unprofessional conduct Short-term emphasis
Positive **Command Climate**	Negative **Command Climate**

Figure 2: Comparison of Great Leader/Tough Boss vs. Toxic Leader. Daniel, T.A. & Metcalf, G.S. (2015). *Crossing the line: An examination of toxic leadership in the U.S. Army.* doi: 10.13140/RG.2.1.2700.4969.

The bottom line: highly effective leaders—whether they are labeled as a great leader or a good one—are clearly concerned about achieving organizational goals *and* they are also focused on developing their people and looking out for the long-term best interests of their organization. The crucial difference is that an ***exceptional*** leader can be distinguished by the ***highly personalized caring*** that they extend to their subordinates (as well as to the families of their people).

Use of Power Orientation

At its core, leadership is about power and influence. Leaders use their power to get things done. While there are numerous types of power and many relevant theories, the theory espoused by McClelland (1975) is most relevant here. He suggests that there are two primary forms of power: *personalized* power—that is, power used for advancing personal gain and influence, and *socialized* power—when the leader's power is used for the benefit of others.

The foundational study for this book supported the theory that both exceptional and tough leaders have a *socialized* power orientation given their willingness to transcend their own self-interest and sacrifice to achieve the mission and collective good of both their people and the organization as a whole.

Impact of Positive Leadership on Organizational Toxicity

The litmus test of a positive leader is the *esprit de corps* they create with their team or division. Positive leaders deliberately increase the flow of positive emotions within their organization. They choose to do this not just because it is a "nice" thing to do for the sake of improving morale, but also because it leads to a measurable increase in performance (Rath, 2014). Studies show that organizational leaders who work to enhance positive emotions have workgroups who share these characteristics: a more positive mood; enhanced job satisfaction; greater engagement; and improved performance.

What differentiates positive leaders from the rest? Instead of being concerned with what they can *get out of* their employees, positive leaders search for opportunities to *invest in* everyone who works for them. They view each interaction with another person as an opportunity to increase his or her positive emotions.

Similar findings about the impact of caring for employees were obtained in a survey of 189,000 employees in 81 diverse organizations as measured by the McKinsey Organizational Health Index (Feser, Mayol, & Srinivasan, 2015). In that study, four key practices statistically explained 89% of the variance in predicting overall leadership effectiveness: (1) supporting others by tuning into how they feel and demonstrating empathetic concern, (2) seeking different perspectives from others, (3) operating with a results orientation, and (4) solving problems effectively.

Overall, the most effective leaders expressed empathetic concern for others by appreciating a person's inherent value, treating others with respect and fairness, affiliating with others, and having a collaborative rather than a competitive orientation. In combination, these practices help to nurture a culture low in organizational toxicity where people can thrive, grow, and do their best work.

Conclusions

The evidence is voluminous and irrefutable that highly personalized caring about people and treating them with dignity and respect is the right thing to do—not only for the benefit of employees and their families, but also for the long-term success of the organization.

Effective leaders know that getting results is critical to the success of their organizations; however, it is those leaders who also excel at *caring for* and *developing their people*—for the long-term—who are truly exceptional. To be sure, these traits can be found in both male and female leaders (but seem to come most naturally for women). As more women are included at the senior-most levels of an organization, it is not difficult to project that the toxicity of our workplace cultures will continue to lessen and improve.

Appendix IV includes additional comments from participants who took part in the research which I hope you will find their experiences with great leaders to be as inspirational as I have!

In addition to caring for and developing their people, exceptional leaders also help to create companies which are profitable and successful, while at the same time work hard to reduce the organizational toxicity that causes employees to quit, mentally check out, or suffer from stress–related emotional or medical conditions. That strikes me as a winning combination by any measure!

References

Army Doctrine Publication 6–22 (2012, August). *Army leadership*. Retrieved from http://Armypubs.Army.mil/doctrine/DR_pubs/dr_a/pdf/ADRP6_22_new.pdf.

Bass, B.M. & Stogdill, R.M. (1990). *Handbook of leadership: A survey of theory and research*. Free Press.

Blake, R.R., & Mouton, J.S. (1964). *The managerial grid*. Gulf Publishing Company.

Blake, R.R., & Mouton, J.S. (1985). *The managerial grid III*. Gulf Publishing Company.

Bowers, D.G. & Seashore, S.E. (1966). Predicting organizational effectiveness with a four–factor theory of leadership. *Administrative Science Quarterly, 11*, 238–263.

Burns, J.M. (1978). *Leadership*. Harper & Row.

Bryman, A., Collinson, D., Grint, K., Jackson, G., & Uhl-Bien, M. (Eds.) (2011). *The SAGE handbook of leadership*. Sage.

Bryman, A. (1992). *Charisma and leadership in organizations*. Sage.

Cartwright, D., & Zander, A. (1960). *Group dynamics research and theory*. Row, Peterson.

Daniel, T.A. & Metcalf, G.S. (2015). *Crossing the line: An examination of toxic leadership in the U.S. Army*. doi: 10.13140/RG.2.1.2700.4969.

Day, D.B. & Antonakis, J. (Eds.) (2012). *The nature of leadership* (2nd ed.). Sage.

Feser, C., Mayol, F. & R. Srinivasan (2015). De-coding leadership: What really matters (2015). *McKinsey Quarterly*. https://www.mckinsey.com/featured-insights/leadership/decoding-leadership-what-really–matters.

Finkelstein, S. (2016). *Superbosses: How exceptional leaders master the flow of talent*. Portfolio/Penguin.

Gardner, J.W. (1990). *On leadership*. Free Press.

Greenleaf, R.K. (1970). *The servant as leader*. The Greenleaf Center for Servant Leadership.

Hemphill, J.K. & Coons, A.E. (1957). Development of the leader behavior description questionnaire. In R.M. Stogdill & A.E. Coons (Eds.), *Leader behavior: Its description and measurement* (Research Monograph No. 99). Ohio State University, Bureau of Business Research.

Hickman, G.R. (Ed.) (2009). *Leading organizations: Perspectives for a new era* (2nd ed.). Sage.

Katz, R.L. (1955). Skills of an effective administrator. *Harvard Business Review, 33*(1), 33–42.

Lord, R.G., DeVader, C.L., & Alliger, G.M. (1986). A meta-analysis of the relationship between personality traits and leadership perceptions: An application of validity generalization procedures. *Journal of Applied Psychology, 71,* 402–410.

Mann, R.D. (1959). A review of the relationship between personality and performance in small groups. *Psychological Bulletin, 56,* 241–270.

McClelland, D.C. (1975). *Power: The inner experience.* Irvington.

Mumford, M.D., Zaccaro, S.J., Harding, F.D., Jacobs, T.O, & Fleishman, E.A. (2000). Leadership skills for a changing world: Solving complex social problems. *Leadership Quarterly, 11*(1), 11–35.

Mumford, M.D. (2006). *Pathways to outstanding leadership: A comparative analysis of charismatic, ideological, and pragmatic leaders.* Lawrence Erlbaum.

Northouse, P.G. (2013). *Leadership: Theory and practice* (6th ed.). Sage.

Rath, T. (2014). The impact of positive leadership. *Gallup.* https://news.gallup.com/businessjournal/11458/impact-positive-leadership.aspx.

Rost, J.C. (1991). *Leadership for the twenty-first century.* Praeger.

Steele, J.P. (2011). Technical Report 2011–3: *Antecedents and consequences of toxic leadership in the U.S. Army: A two-year review and recommended solutions.* Center for Army Leadership. http://usacac.Army.mil/CAC2/Repository/CASAL_TechReport2011-3_ToxicLeadership.pdf.

Stogdill, R.M. (1948). Personal factors associated with leadership: A survey of the literature. *Journal of Psychology, 25,* 35–71.

Stogdill, R.M. (1974). *Handbook of leadership: A survey of theory and research.* Free Press.

Additional Suggested Reading

Bennis, W. & Nanus, B. (1985). *Leaders: The strategies for taking charge.* Harper & Row.

George, B. (2007). *True north: Discover your authentic leadership.* Jossey-Bass.

Levinson, H. (2006). *On the psychology of leadership.* Harvard Business School Publishing Corporation.

Northouse, P.G. (2019). *Leadership: Theory and practice.* Sage.

Rath, T. & Conchie, B. (2008). *Strengths based leadership: Great leaders, teams, and why people follow.* Gallup Press.

Stein, S.J. (2017). *The EQ leader: Instilling passion, creating shared goals, and building meaningful organizations through emotional intelligence.* John Wiley & Sons.

Ulrich, D., Zenger, J. & N. Smallwood (1999). *Results-based leadership: How leaders build the business and improve the bottom line.* Harvard Business School Press.

Organizational Toxicity: Factors Which Promote Toxic Behavior

Chapter 5
Societal Factors: Social Systems and Expectations That Contribute to the Development of Toxic Leaders

Sadly, my work over the past three decades has demonstrated that employees are not always respected at work, nor are they always shielded or protected by the policies, laws, regulations, and systems that organizations and government institutions have put in place to protect them. Although much has been done, there is still much left to do. I hope you will be persuaded by the research and arguments presented in this book to join me in my continued efforts to create a kinder, gentler workplace.

A large volume of the toxicity that currently exists within organizations is caused by leaders who engage in what I think of as the "toxic trio" of abuse—sexual assault, sexual harassment, and workplace bullying. What I have come to believe and understand is this: (1) most workplace misconduct is actually an abuse of power—it's not really about sex at all; (2) these problems are most definitely not just "women's issues" because they eventually affect us all; and (3) the problems persist because there are typically no consequences for the perpetrator. When these conditions are present, toxic leaders are not only allowed to engage in these abusive behaviors, but they tend to thrive and teach others how to manipulate and abuse employees by their example.

Organizational problems like these do not exist in a vacuum, though. It is inevitable that society's problems will spill over to the workplace. Here is what credible evidence tells us about what is happening to our mothers, spouses, daughters, sisters, and granddaughters—in their homes, while they are away at college, and in their workplaces:

Sexual Violence

According to the Rape, Abuse, and Incest National Network (n.d.):
§ One out of every 6 American women has been the target of an attempted or completed rape in her lifetime (14.8% completed and 2.8% attempted). This compares to an attempted or completed rape of one of every 33 American men (3%). On average, there are 433,648 targets of rape and sexual assault each year in the U.S. against targets age 12 or older. In 93% of these incidents, the target knows the perpetrator (59% acquaintance or 34% family member), while only 7% were strangers.
§ Sexual violence on college campuses is similarly pervasive. 23.1% of female and 5.4% of male undergraduate students experience rape or sexual assault through physical force, violence, or incapacitation. 21% of TGQN (transgender, gender queer, nonconforming) college students have been sexually assaulted, compared to 18% of non-TGQN females and 4% of non-TGQN males. However, only 20% of female col-

https://doi.org/10.1515/9783111201771-005

lege-age students between the ages of 18 and 24 report the assault to law enforcement.

§ The staggering reality is that every 73 seconds, a sexual assault is committed in the U.S. (and every 9 minutes that target is a child), but only 5 of every 1,000 rapists will ever end up in prison.

Sexual Harassment

§ Sexual harassment has been illegal since 1980 when the Equal Employment Opportunity Commission (EEOC) issued regulations stating it was a form of sex discrimination prohibited by the Civil Rights Act of 1964 (U.S. Equal Employment Opportunity Commission, n.d.). Corporations have issued anti-harassment policies and offered training and communication about the issue on an annual basis for some time, but the problem persists unabated.

§ In the 2018 survey by *Stop Street Harassment* (2018), a nationally representative survey of men and women over the age of 18, 81% of the participating women and 43% of the men reported experiencing some form of sexual harassment in their lifetime. In addition, 77% of the women reported being subjected to verbal harassment, 51% reported having been physically touched without their permission, and 41% reported being sexually harassed online. Despite the prevalence of the problem, though, the EEOC estimates that fewer than 14% of these individuals ever file a formal complaint (Smith, 2018).

Workplace Bullying

§ Workplace bullying is defined by the U.S. Workplace Bullying Institute (WBI) as "repeated mistreatment, abusive conduct that is threatening, intimidating, or humiliating; work sabotage; or verbal abuse" (Workplace Bullying Institute, 2021). In the latest national survey by WBI in 2021, 30% of Americans reported that they have suffered abusive conduct at work, and another 19% have witnessed it—that's 79.3 million American workers who are affected by workplace bullying, both directly and indirectly.

§ The target of bullying is female in 49% of all cases, while 67% of all bullies are men. And as with sexual assaults and sexual harassment, the national survey data shows that targets typically do not report the situation and when they do, 60% received a negative reaction from their employer who faulted them for their "ineffective reactions". Employer responses to an official complaint of abuse included encouragement, denial, rationalization, defense of abuse, and discounting.

Reasons Why Incidents Go Unreported

How can this possibly be, you might be asking? The best answer that I can provide to you is this: when incidents of sexual assault, sexual harassment, and workplace bullying happen, targets typically do not report the incident and there are rarely any consequences for the perpetrator.

So why do these situations so often go unreported? Here are some of the most common responses given when targets are asked this question:
- because they need their job and paycheck (and the perpetrator is often their boss);
- because they want to protect their reputation and fear their friends and families will blame them for somehow causing the incident;
- because they fear they will not be believed;
- because they have no confidence that anything will be done to change the situation for the better;
- because they fear retaliation; and/or
- in the very worst-case scenario, all the above.

You can quickly see that the likelihood of *"institutional betrayal"*— when the organization fails to respect the aggrieved person's concerns, blames them for causing the problem, or openly questions their truthfulness—are strong motivators for deciding not to report an incident. Based on the usual outcomes of these situations, these fears are quite legitimate. You have likely seen it happen in your own workplace (despite your best intentions). The truth is that the situation rarely ever turns out well for the target.

A prominent and memorable case in point: former President Trump's mocking of Dr. Christine Blasey Ford's testimony in 2018 about her alleged sexual assault to the Senate Judiciary Committee considering the nomination to the U.S. Supreme Court of Brett Kavanaugh (Haberman & Baker, 2018). This situation alone has likely served to convince most American women that not only will they not be believed, they run the risk of being publicly taunted and humiliated if they dare to come forward with allegations of misconduct against a powerful man (even if they are highly educated, articulate, and provide credible allegations). And, in cases like Dr. Ford's, there is a real potential for having their lives (and those of their families) threatened. The fear is not imagined.

Do you see a pattern here? The perpetrator relies on his targets not to report his misconduct (and based on the statistics, it's a pretty safe bet). If they do file a complaint, he admits to nothing, and then blames his target by accusing her of lying, for "bringing it on," or that it was actually consensual sex.

So, there you have it. The target is often not believed, or she is retaliated against, or she gets fired—*a perfect trifecta of injustice*—resulting in yet more psychological trauma. And the end result? Nothing about the situation changes for the better for the target and there are no real consequences for the abuser. Is it any wonder, then, that most women decide that it is futile to report incidents of sexual assault, sexual harassment, or workplace bullying?

Possible Solutions

We need to change this situation—and we need to change it fast. So, let's get serious about promoting more women to senior-level leadership positions in order to provide a better balance of leadership styles and approaches.

And let's stop with the *"himpathy"*—what Cornell philosophy professor Kate Manne brilliantly defines as "the inappropriate and disproportionate sympathy powerful men often enjoy in cases of sexual assault, intimate partner violence, homicide, and other misogynistic behavior" (Manne, 2018). It is a pathology within our society that causes people, both men and women, to favor the more powerful man and excuse his bad behavior.

We have all heard the exculpatory phrase *"boys will be boys"*. It happens way too often and is problematic on multiple fronts (*People v. Turner*, Wikipedia, n.d.). It allows bad behavior to go unpunished, it disrespects the target, and it trivializes the potential seriousness of the incident.

"Himpathizers" tend to believe that all women who report an incident of sexual assault, sexual harassment, or workplace bullying are opportunistic liars, which is simply not the case (Manne, 2018). In fact, a review of the research puts false reporting of sexual violence between 2 and 10% (National Sexual Violence Resource Center, n.d.). This suggests that the vast majority of women who come forward with an allegation of misconduct against a more powerful man are actually telling the truth.

Let me be clear: These are multifaceted and complex problems, and there are no simple solutions. However, there are research-based intervention strategies that have been proven to be effective—teaching people to become *active bystanders*. This type of training teaches witnesses to actively intervene where an incident of assault or abuse may be occurring or where someone may be at risk. *Green Dot*, offered through Alteristic, is among the finest of the bystander programs currently available. They offer evidence-based prevention and intervention strategies and training across the human lifespan (Green Dot Program, n.d.).

The reason that bystander training can be effective is because most people are not abusive or mean-spirited. There are far more people who don't want people to be harmed than there are people who choose to engage in the harm. My point is that if we all commit to share accountability for keeping each other safe, it is possible for the situation to actually shift in a positive direction.

Applying this approach to our workplaces could be helpful too. By providing clear expectations about behavior, communicating those expectations regularly, training staff about bystander strategies, and rewarding compliance with those standards, we can help to motivate bystanders at work to act appropriately to the situation to help stop the abuse and, importantly, let the target know they are not alone.

The ultimate goal would be to ensure that everyone in the organization is prepared to stand up for the safety and equality of everyone at work. When this shift happens, the perpetrators will simply not be permitted to get away with acts of misconduct—not because senior leaders have intervened or because company policy requires it—but because their co-workers will simply not allow it.

When employees feel that their company is fair and just, they are much more likely to help a victimized colleague (Priesemuth, 2020). Also, a greater sense of accountability is likely to occur among all employees when they start to believe that they really can make a positive difference (Sanderson, 2020).

Although this approach has not yet been widely adopted by corporate America, it can be anticipated that its use will grow. It is currently being used effectively on college campuses (Green Dot for Colleges, n.d.), in the military (Hollaback!, n.d.), and by numerous nonprofit organizations (Smith, 2018). It is also recommended as a promising "best practice" by the U.S. Equal Employment Opportunity Commission for use by American employers (Equal Employment Opportunity Commission, n.d.).

We will most definitely need training—and, most importantly courage—to learn how to safely intervene in these situations. In the wise words of former First Lady Michelle Obama (2011):

> You may not always have a comfortable life, and you will not always be able to solve all of the world's problems at once, but don't ever underestimate the importance you can have because history has shown us that courage can be contagious and hope can take on a life of its own.

A permissive environment provides the perfect conditions for toxic leaders to flourish. Our institutions have betrayed both men and women by not holding perpetrators accountable for their misconduct, either in our society-at-large or in our workplaces. If they had, these problems would have ended a long time ago.

So that means it's up to all of us: senior leaders, HR practitioners, supervisors, and employees—all of us working in concert. We must end our passive silence and begin actively standing up for targets—even if it means getting involved in difficult and messy situations we would rather avoid. It's time for all of us to *see something, say something, do something.*

References

GreenDot for Colleges (n.d.) https://alteristic.org/services/green-dot/green-dot-colleges/.

Hollaback! (n.d.) *The 5 D's of responding as a bystander*. https://www.ihollaback.org/resources/bystander-resources/.

Haberman, M. & Baker, P. (2018, October 2). Trump taunts Christine Blasey Ford at rally. *New York Times*. https://www.nytimes.com/2018/10/02/us/politics/trump-me-too.html.

Manne, K. (2018). *Brett Kavanaugh and America's "himpathy" reckoning*. https://www.nytimes.com/2018/09/26/opinion/brett-kavanaugh-hearing-himpathy.html?smid=fb-nytimes&smtyp=cur.

National Sexual Violence Resource Center (n.d.). *False reporting*. https://www.nsvrc.org/sites/default/files/Publications_NSVRC_Overview_False-Reporting.pdf.

Obama, M. (2011). Remarks by the first lady during keynote address at young African women leader's forum. *Office of the White House Press Release*. https://obamawhitehouse.archives.gov/the-press-office/2011/06/22/remarks-first-lady-during-keynote-address-young-african-women-leaders-fo.

People v. Turner, Wikipedia (n.d.). https://en.wikipedia.org/wiki/People_v._Turner.Brock Turner was a Stanford University swimmer convicted of three counts of felony sexual assault against a female while she was unconscious. Turner was sentenced to only six months in jail and three years of probation. He was also required to register as a sex offender and undergo rehabilitation. The judge in the case, Aaron Persky, explained the lenient sentence by stating that he *"didn't want to ruin the boy's life."*

Priesemuth, M. (2020, June 19). Time's up for toxic workplaces. *Harvard Business Review*. https://hbr.org/2020/06/times-up-for-toxic-workplaces.

Rape, Abuse, and Incest National Network. https://www.rainn.org/about-sexual-assault.

Sanderson, C.A. (2020). *Why we act: Turning bystanders into moral rebels*. The Belknap Press of Harvard University Press.

Smith, B.L. (2018, February). *What it really takes to stop sexual harassment*. American Psychological Association. https://www.apa.org/monitor/2018/02/sexual-harassment.aspx.

Stop Street Harassment (2018). *2018 study on sexual harassment and assault*. http://www.stopstreetharassment.org/resources/2018-national-sexual-abuse-report/.

U.S. Equal Employment Opportunity Commission (n.d.). *Statistics on sexual harassment*. https://www.eeoc.gov/eeoc/statistics/enforcement/sexual_harassment_new.cfm.

U.S. Equal Employment Opportunity Commission (n.d.) *Best practices for employers and HR/EEO professionals*. https://www.eeoc.gov/eeoc/initiatives/e-race/bestpractices-employers.cfm.

Workplace Bullying Institute (WBI) *2021 U.S. Workplace Bullying Study* (2021). https://workplacebullying.org/2021-wbi-survey/.

Workplace Bullying Institute (WBI) *2021 U.S. Workplace Bullying Study* (2021). https://workplacebullying.org/2021-wbi-survey/.

Chapter 6
Conducive Workplace Climate: Organizational Factors That Promote Bad Behavior

It is not hard to see how societal issues influence the development of toxic and abusive leaders who end up contaminating our workspaces, but societal issues are just one part of a multi-headed problem. In this chapter we will explore how people, policies, and practices conspire, whether intentionally or inadvertently, to create the "conducive climate" at work which helps to drive bad behavior. If there are no consequences to abusive actions, the clear message to employees from the organization is that bad behavior is a necessary evil required to attain results.

In most corporate settings, there is a relentless pressure to achieve financial goals; however, there are typically no rewards or recognition for being a "nice guy" who treats employees with kindness, compassion, or empathy. The idea that "what gets measured gets done" tends to pervade organizational life—and we all know that what gets measured are goals related to efficiency, productivity, and profitability.

We will next examine some of the most common components of a "conducive climate"—an organizational environment lacking in accountability and in which toxic leaders can thrive.

Lack of Inclusion of Women at Senior Levels

An imbalance of men and women in the workplace can lead to a situation where certain types of aggressive (and often dysfunctional) behaviors can inadvertently become the accepted norm. Working to create a more inclusive environment—one with a more equal balance of both men and women leaders—can help to ensure that there are many different types of leader styles and approaches for employees to emulate and from which they can learn.

Senior Leaders Are Unaware of, or Ambivalent Toward, the Problem

Toxic leaders tend to "kiss up" as they "kick down" (VanKleef, Homan, Finkenauer, Gundemir, & Stamkon, 2011). They work hard to please their superiors while at the same time treating their subordinates badly; as a result, they are frequently well-liked by senior management (Sutton, 2007). This partially explains why their superiors so often fail to realize that their leadership style is a problem.

https://doi.org/10.1515/9783111201771-006

Either they don't see it or they're just happy to get the results that come from that person and maybe they're too busy to really pay attention . . . and you know we've got these values of loyalty and duty, so you do the hard work and you don't want to whine, I guess.

Conversely, the senior leader may be aware of the situation but not consider the behaviors to be problematic or actionable because the individual is getting results and, in turn, making the senior officer look good, resulting in promotions and benefits up the chain of command too.

Lack of Accountability for the Development of Subordinates

Despite the importance and value to both employees and the organization, many leaders simply do not make it a priority to engage in mentoring, coaching, counseling, or providing performance feedback to their subordinates. The most frequent excuses given include a lack of accountability for those who do not counsel, not enough time available, lack of knowledge and skills, and leader avoidance of situations that might lead to interpersonal conflict.

Importantly, there is generally no recognition or reward for leaders who emphasize the human dimension of leadership. Importantly, there are also no consequences for those who are so self-interested that they fail to help develop the next generation of leaders coming up behind them.

So, I just think in the culture that we have [in most organizations], it's "What have you done for me lately?" and rarely is it "Have you made my people better?"

The development of others is not often stressed as a leader's priority. As a result, promotions sometimes occur too early and based on *potential* (and not proven ability)—and often well before a person is really ready to assume the role. The increased responsibility, coupled with a lack of readiness, can push an individual far outside of his comfort zone, making him more susceptible to adopting a toxic style due to the increased stress of the new responsibilities.

"Toxic Migration" to Other Parts of the Organization

When senior leaders are aware of the problems and *do* get involved, they often resort to a "restructuring" strategy and simply reassign the toxic leader (who is at that point a known liability) to another location—a practice commonly referred to as "toxic migration" (Milligan, 2020).

This response is problematic because there is no action taken to either coach the individual to change or to remove them from their leadership post. The result is that the organization enables the behavior by failing to stop it, sending an implicit—and dangerous—message to the organization that it is an acceptable way to operate.

> One thing that always ticked me off with the senior leaders I've worked for is that they will be in private conversation and say, "See that guy over there? That guy never should have been [promoted]". I say, "Why not, sir?" And they would say, "Because he was a toxic leader or he was incompetent". And I'd say "Well, didn't he work for you at one time?" And he's says, "Yes, he worked for me". And I'd ask, "Well, why didn't you take him out?" And their answer is always, well, "It's not really my job to do that, the institution has to do that". And I've always called their bluff and said, "Bullshit. You are the institution. If you don't make a statement about that person's potential, who will?" And now because you haven't, they continue to move up the ranks and you passed the buck onto someone else.

> a lot of times they'll promote them [the toxic leader] just to get them out of the unit. They'll promote the guy really quick and say what a great job he's doing—it's called "dumping the fat". They'll go promote him to get him out of the way so somebody else that's a good leader can come in.

What happens in too many organizations is a proverbial "pass the buck" situation where the toxic leader is promoted and dumped on another department or subsidiary —becoming at that point "someone else's problem". The result is that the toxic leader is not confronted about the problem or coached to change so he may never really understand the nature of his negative behavior on others. Paradoxically, because he is rewarded for these very behaviors, it is highly likely that he will continue to repeat them given the personal success such tactics have consistently generated for him.

Organizational Culture Which Values Loyalty and Discourages Reporting

Most of us are taught early in our careers that loyalty and respect for authority are key virtues. This way of thinking makes subordinates unlikely to question the leader's power and authority or to report irregularities despite numerous available organizational channels to do so. This loyalty factor also makes people highly reluctant to bypass the chain of command to report a toxic leader to a more senior one. As a result, many employees simply "take it" and/or decide to "wait it out" because they do not want to appear disloyal, be labeled as a "troublemaker", or embarrass their group by identifying to others that their leader is "toxic" (Aubrey, 2012).

> Really, your only option is to appeal to the higher level [leader] which is also kind of the "nuclear option" . . . It's very easy with a wink and a nudge to stall out someone's career. So, if you are willing to make the jump and go to the next-level leader to talk about the situation which involves your direct supervisor, then you're assuming a great deal of risk.

This sense of loyalty and reluctance to report problems in the corporate sector has a corollary. It can be compared to the "blue wall of silence" observed by police officers (Wikipedia, n.d.). This is a term used to denote an unwritten rule that implicitly exists among police officers where they agree amongst themselves not to report on a colleague's errors, misconduct, or crimes.

If officially questioned about an incident of misconduct involving another officer, the officer being questioned will claim ignorance of another officer's wrongdoing. The code is observed, ostensibly, to keep loyalty intact and so that an officer is not viewed as a "traitor", a "maverick", or as a "boat rocker". Their chief concern is that if they do report a situation, they will find themselves in a difficult situation in the field —one that fails to include adequate backup or support should reprisal be the preferred form of payback for their perceived disloyalty.

Most organizations observe an "open-door" policy and some have formal processes (e.g., ombudsperson, etc.) that provide employees with alternative channels where they can address concerns. However, there is also a general expectation that problems should first be discussed within one's direct chain of command.

> So you have several routes to report things; however, a lot of people . . . are hesitant to do that because they're afraid to be labeled as a "troublemaker". So at the same time where a senior leader will say, "My door is always open . . .", they will then say, "However, I highly encourage you to utilize your chain of command first."

It is no surprise, then, that these expectations often have a chilling effect on reporting. People are reluctant to risk their careers and create financial instability for themselves and their families (e.g., reduction and/or elimination of pay, benefits, and retirement plan) by being labeled a "troublemaker" or "whistleblower" and they clearly have good and valid reasons to worry.

> It's easy to "fall on your sword" when you are single and you can you know go back to school or spend a couple years backpacking through Europe . . . but when you've got family to support, it turns good people. It makes good people much more willing to look the other way. Even in my situation, I'll admit that I tolerated the [bad] behavior longer because I was recently married and I was worried about taking care of my wife.

> You just don't want to get labeled [as a "troublemaker" or not a team player] by reporting a toxic leader or going around him. That would be career suicide.

As a result, "not making waves" and "waiting it out" are viewed as viable options given the high personal stakes involved. They also worry that if they report the individual and nothing is done, they will be penalized once the toxic leader becomes aware of their complaint and end up in even worse shape.

> I mean you could probably go over their head, but the chances of something being fixed compared to the possibility of your life drastically changing if you went over the head of your direct line boss and nothing happened . . . it just wouldn't be worth it.

Though there are clearly internal avenues available to report a toxic leader, these processes are not really considered to be truly viable options.

Trying to deal with a toxic leader is kind of like trying to throw a grenade over a wall. You might make it, but then if you don't, you know it's going to be bad.

Without an intent to cast blame, it should be noted that employees also play a role in the dynamic. Without their silence and/or failure to report the issue, toxic leaders would quickly become powerless. Silent subordinates are the enablers that help to allow toxic leaders to operate without consequence, but it is a big "ask" to expect them to put their livelihoods and paychecks on the line when the consequences are so high.

Imitation of Successful Leaders Who are Toxic

Individuals tend to pay close attention to how senior leaders in the organization operate and how they treat their subordinates. Based on a desire to achieve similar professional success, those who are relatively new in their careers often imitate the same attitudes and behaviors that they see being rewarded. As a result of this imitation, these people are inadvertently trained to become the next generation of toxic leaders.

There is a saying that your boss dictates your experience, your mood, so I rarely think that the individual sees themselves as toxic . . . I think this is just what they've known. This is the culture they've grown up in and they just are a byproduct of the people who came before them in many cases, and I mean I'll tell you I think there are a lot more toxic leaders than there are nontoxic leaders.

Borrowing from a psychodynamic notion of "identification with the aggressor", the subordinate may assume the attributes of the toxic leader so that he transforms from the person threatened into the person who makes the threat. This defense mechanism protects him from the anxiety caused by the toxic leader.

People see that the yellers and screamers are the ones getting promoted—because that's what most people look toward is who's getting promoted. If you look on that list and it's like toxic, toxic, toxic, well you know what, "Forget this, I've got to feed my family". This is my life. [My career] is based on how high I make it. So, if I've got to piss you off so I can have my big mansion on the hill well, guess what, I'm going to piss you off.

Organizational Culture with Low Perceived Risk and No Consequences

Bad behavior often occurs when the perpetrator assesses the costs of engaging in those behaviors as being relatively small. The costs involve the risk of getting a reprimand or being fired (which they typically perceive as low), while the benefits can be higher pay, bonuses, promotions, and increasing levels of power and influence.

If there are no policies against abusive tactics, no monitoring, and no punishment, a reasonable interpretation is that the organization simply accepts it as a legitimate leadership style (O'Leary-Kelly, Griffin, & Glew, 1996). When this is the case, a possible perpetrator will then perceive the costs and dangers of engaging in such actions as very low.

There also seems to be an association between abusive behavior and leadership style. In an organization with a laissez faire ("hands off") style of leadership, it is reasonable to assume that weak leaders will not be aware of the issues so they will seldom intervene or respond to reports of abusive behaviors. Similarly, it is reasonable to assume that the risk of discipline or other consequences is also low. As a result, it becomes a useful strategy when it can be reasonably expected that leaders will not do anything to stop it.

Clearly, most organizations do not intend to create an environment where toxic leaders flourish, and most do have some level of checks and balances. However, a failure to rein in a toxic leader early for their negative tactics enables toxic leaders—allowing them to remain under the radar and continue to be promoted.

> *I've seen climates that are so palpable—it's like a building with no ventilation. You're like, "Jeez, I need to get out of here. This is bad. Morale is bad." And then the moment they're gone [the toxic leader], everything changes 100%.*

The bottom line is that abusive leaders see no reason *not* to use aggressive and abusive tactics because all too often there are no consequences for doing so. Conversely, the potential rewards can be quite significant resulting in a risk-reward situation that is evaluated in favor of taking the risk.

Competition for Promotions, Influence and Rewards Encourages Toxic Behavior

Though perhaps unintended, there are actually a lot of good reasons that a person might choose to use abusive tactics at work. When individuals strive to be promoted, have influence, and acquire resources—referred to as *micro-political behavior*—it is not surprising that they would use competitive behaviors to get ahead. In fact, these behaviors might be the most "rational" of all forms of workplace aggression given that seeking to be successful through the achievement of promotions, rewards, and/or influence is generally accepted as a "reasonable" workplace motive.

> *We have a system where people are forced to outperform their peers constantly. [Consequently], they will exert that pressure that is being placed on them to their subordinates. And "to hell" with their subordinates—because it's all about them [the toxic leader and his personal gain]. Our hierarchical system and kind of linear career progression means that people are looking for opportunities to get a quick advantage so that they can get that next promotion a year ahead of their peers. There is a concern that people are going to become backstabbing as things gets more competitive. I think most people will try to stand out on their own as opposed to helping others.*

Moreover, when pay or bonuses are based on a relative ranking of employees, an individual may be more motivated to abuse colleagues and subordinates. In fact, by sabotaging the work of a colleague, the perpetrator may improve his or her own standing (Treadway, Shaughnessy, Breland, Yang, & Reeves, 2013). In addition, if an employee is evaluated based on the performance of the team to which he belongs, he may strategically want to expel very low performing team members who could negatively impact his pay or bonus.

It is also possible to see how the adoption of abusive tactics may simply be an efficient way to get things done—a productive part of organizational life that helps to progress the strategic mission. These tactics are sometimes used to drive unwanted employees out of the corporation who might otherwise be difficult to legally terminate, or they might be used strategically to terminate an employee to avoid severance payments.

Summing It Up

All too often, individuals are rewarded solely for achieving their strategic goals and their organizations do not penalize them for the destruction and demoralization of people in their path along the way. Leaders who essentially operate without regard for others often successfully navigate the social and political environment and achieve high performance ratings, suggesting that there is a functional and rational perspective associated with the use of bad behavior at work. Assuming this to be true, it is a sad, but true, indictment of the current condition of too many of our 21st century workplaces.

References

Aubrey, D.W. (2012). *The effect of toxic leadership.* U.S. Army War College. http://www.au.af.mil/au/awc/awc gate/Army-usawc/aubrey_toxic_leadership.pdf.

Milligan, S. (2020). When a toxic worker is well-liked by managers. *SHRM.* https://www.shrm.org/resource sandtools/hr-topics/employee-relations/pages/when-a-toxic-worker-is-well-liked-by-managers.aspx.

O'Leary-Kelly, A.M., Griffin, R.W. & Glew, D.J. (1996). Organization-motivated aggression: A research framework. *Academy of Management Review, 21*(1), 225–253.

Sutton, R. (2007). *The no asshole rule: Building a civilized workplace and surviving one that isn't.* Warner Business Books.

Treadway, D.C., Shaughnessy, B.A., Breland, J.W., Yang, J. & Reeves, M. (2013). Political skill and the job performance of bullies. *Journal of Managerial Psychology, 28* (3), 273–289.

VanKleef, M. Homan, G.A., Finkenauer, A.C., Gundemir, S., & Stamkon, E. (2011). Breaking the rules to rise to power: How norm violators gain power in the eyes of others. *Social Psychological and Personality Science, 2*(5), 500–507.

Wikipedia (n.d.). *The blue wall of silence.* https://en.wikipedia.org/wiki/Blue_wall_of_silence.

Chapter 7
Ethical Temptations at the Top: Executive Success and the Increased Potential for Ethical Failure

Not only do our workplaces create opportunities where bad behavior is often rewarded, but we live in a society that makes celebrities of successful people in sports, politics, business and government only to find that they are not really what they have advertised themselves to be. With only a cursory scan of recent news reports, it is very easy to identify many more high-profile people who have been involved in very public scandals in recent years. Donald J. Trump, the twice impeached and four times criminally indicted former President of the United States, immediately comes to mind (Wikipedia, n.d.; Sullivan & Olson, 2023).

It is becoming increasingly difficult to find leaders who can sustain our respect over the course of a long and distinguished career. This is especially true in a world that can publicly broadcast indiscretions or misdeeds with almost lightning speed. Tragically, the list of executives who have been involved in spectacular falls from grace seems almost endless.

Accounting fraud, embezzlement, tax evasion, bid rigging, over-billing, substance abuse, sexual impropriety, and perjury top the list of indiscretions most frequently leading to the downfall of successful business executives. Leaders who were at one time the focus of admiration by the press regularly appear on the cover of business magazines reporting on their removal from senior positions with headlines like *"Flameout"* or *"What Went Wrong?"* Others face messy public trials, government investigations, corporate audits, and/or costly divorces for their actions. The public is no longer surprised by reports of these reckless acts; sadly, we have almost come to expect them.

There are numerous personal and organizational benefits that typically go along with success: increasing levels of power, influence, rewards, status, and control of resources. However, history confirms that high-level achievement can often come with a fairly hefty price tag (Kelly, 1988). Paradoxically, it is at the very height of their careers that leaders become the most vulnerable to ethical or moral lapses. Just when it appears (at least to those on the outside) that they "have it all", they often engage in risky behaviors that blow it all up.

It is the intent of this chapter to explore this paradox of success as it applies to business leaders who then often become toxic leaders at a time when they have just achieved major professional success. We will more closely examine why highly intelligent people are often seduced into taking more risks and making poor decisions just when they have achieved great organizational success and have the most to lose. In addition, strategic recommendations will be provided that can help both individuals and organizations avoid these costly leadership failures.

https://doi.org/10.1515/9783111201771-007

What Makes Leaders Fail?

Privileged Access

When a person becomes highly successful at work, he or she typically gains greater power and influence, increased status (both internally and externally), a heightened sense of personal achievement, plus greater perks and financial rewards. These personal benefits of success are collectively referred to as *privileged access* (Ludwig & Longenecker, 1993). In addition to these personal gains, the successful leader generally is given include greater control of resources and decision processes, increased access to information, people and resources, and the ability to set their own agendas without direct day-to-day supervision.

Lack of Balance

As corporate executives climb the corporate ladder, an inability to share their problems, hopes and dreams, coupled with large blocks of time away from home, can cause them to experience a sense of increasing personal isolation and a lack of intimacy in their relationships (Berglas, 1986). It can also lead them to become somewhat out of touch with reality (Kets de Vries, 1989).

I Want it All—And I Want it Now

As leaders become more successful, they frequently become more "emotionally expansive" with an almost insatiable appetite for increased markers of success, thrills, gratification, and control (Blotnick, 1987). Jim Collins refers to it as *"the undisciplined pursuit of more"* (Collins, 2009). Once this level of success has been achieved, executives often lose their ability to be satisfied with their current status and desire more and more of the trappings of success (e.g., a McMansion in the most exclusive gated neighborhood, expensive cars and jewelry, private schools for their children, customized boats, second or third homes, etc.).

Stress and a Heightened Fear of Failure

Once successful, leaders often become increasingly stressed and fearful about not achieving their goals, leading to constant anxiety and concern about the future (Ludwig & Longenecker, 1993). Coupled with the increasing isolation commonly experienced as a byproduct of organizational success, executives can find themselves in a very lonely and discontented situation. All too often, their loneliness and sense of isolation are not off set by the tangible rewards and status associated with their position.

Inflated Ego and a Sense of Exemption from Rules

All of the trappings that come with corporate success can collude to make a leader develop an "inflated sense of personal ability to manipulate outcomes" (Ludwig & Longenecker, 1993). This egocentricity can cause the leader to become abrasive, close-minded, disrespectful, and prone to extreme displays of negative emotion. This sense of personal infallibility has been referred to as the *"I am the center of the universe phenomenon"* (Blotnick, 1987).

A similar phenomenon has been confirmed by Price (2006, 2000) who suggested that leadership induces and maintains a leader's belief that they are somehow exempt from the moral requirements that apply to the rest of us. This can cause a leader to subconsciously develop a belief that while there is a mandatory set of rules for most people, there is a different (and less restrictive) set of rules which govern him.

The "Emptiness Syndrome"

After working for years and finally achieving senior levels of responsibility and all that comes with it, leaders often take a step back and ask themselves, *"Is this all there is?"* (Conger, 1990). When they have exceeded their own career expectations in terms of position, pay, and perks, there is little else left for them to strive for on a professional level. These are typically hard-charging executives who have been engaged in a relentless pursuit of goals and results during their entire career. If there is nothing left to strive for, they often stop and ask themselves, *"What's the point?"*

When this happens, the lack of new goals can undermine the early clarity of purpose that led to their success in the first place. It is at that point that boredom can set in which can stimulate the executive to take more risks or become distracted from focusing on the work of the organization.

Early Strengths Become Later Weaknesses

Jay Conger (1990) suggested that most people experience a duality in their lives. Steve Jobs, the now-deceased former CEO and founder of Apple, is a recent example of a very public business leader with a prominent duality attached to his legacy. In fact, the August 2012 cover of *Wired* magazine shows a photograph of Jobs sporting both a halo and horns along with a provocative story title that read: *"Do you **really** want to be like Steve Jobs?"* (Austen, 2012).

According to those who knew him best, he was a brilliant innovator; to others, he was a tyrant and a jerk. Apparently, both perspectives were absolutely on target depending on the situation and the person. As a result, his life story serves as an inspiration for some and a cautionary tale for others. It is the very strengths that a leader is treasured and admired for that can become a liability under the right circumstances, especially during times of stress (Conger, 1990; McIntosh & Rima, 1997). These potential but latent weaknesses have often been referred to as "the dark side of leadership" (LaBier, 1986).

It is often at the top that an executive will self-destruct by taking action that they know is perilous, yet they arrogantly believe that they have the power to conceal it and not get caught. So, despite the acknowledged risk, they engage in the dangerously risky action anyway. Why? Either the leader becomes bored and arrogantly expects that the misdeeds will not be discovered or becomes convinced that it is his deserved repayment for prior sacrifices (Ciulla, 2004; Ciulla, 1998).

Ironically, it is the most successful leaders that tend to suffer the worst ethical dilemmas (Boddy, 2011). Equally ironic is the fact that most leaders dethroned by scandal have a long and distinguished history of honest and loyal service to their organization (Maccoby, 2003). This is why their precipitous falls from grace are generally so shocking and unexpected to those who know them well.

Corporate Culture Drives Bad Behaviors

Some industries seem to be based on a culture of greed and excess: as an example, think Wall Street. The finance industry represents capitalism in its purest form—the single-minded pursuit of profit. As the 2008 financial crisis confirmed, it appears that our financial structure is predicated on a system which colludes to drive bad behavior (Greycourt, 2008). It is a system based on poor risk controls, massive leverage, egregious financial rewards, predatory lending practices, the purchase of influence, and a complete lack of any sense of fiduciary responsibility to the ultimate client (Nielsen, 1987).

Many commentators have suggested that the root cause of the crisis was the gradual collapse of ethical behavior across the financial industry. Financial firms began to behave in ways that were in their (and especially their top executives) short-term interest without any concern about the longer-term impact on the industry's customers, on the broader economy, or even on the firm's own employees.

Within such a context, it is relatively easy to understand the significant temptation that exists for executives to make decisions that have the potential to increase their personal bonuses and rewards, but which are not necessarily in their client or organization's best interest.

Strategies to Help Minimize Potential Ethical Failures

Calamitous ethical failures happen with an alarming frequency as a byproduct of great success. As a result, it is prudent for organizations to consider taking steps to help minimize these risks (Moore, Detert, Klebe Trevino, Baker, & Mayer, 2012). Suggested ways to set up guardrails to deter ethical infractions include:

Individual Support Mechanisms

Guardrails directly aimed at supporting individuals include:
- **Establish an ethical culture** by ensuring that the senior leadership team consists of seasoned and professional executives who will both challenge and support each other as needs dictate.
- **Ensure an inclusive and balanced level of men and women working in senior positions** to ensure that there are a variety of leadership styles and approaches for employees to emulate and from which they can learn.
- **Provide 360-degree performance feedback to executives** to give them input about their performance from a variety of perspectives (e.g., boss, peers, and subordinates). This type of multi-rater system can help ensure that any perceived deficiencies are quickly identified and discussed with the executive.
- **Use coaching** to teach leaders how to recognize the types of situations that are likely to magnify their weaknesses, along with coping strategies to mitigate these potential issues.
- **Ensure that the senior leaders have strong and independent staffs** and employees at all levels within the organization who will not hesitate to disagree or discuss alternative points of view. As leaders become more successful, there is an increasing danger that they will attempt to surround themselves with "yes" people who do not challenge or provide them with candid feedback and information that would help in their overall decision making.
- **Communicate about integrity and key organizational policies and expectations at key career moments** (e.g., promotions, expansion of job responsibilities, etc.) as these are also times during which executives are vulnerable to risky behaviors and/or ethical lapses.
- **Establish (and enforce) work/family policies** that promote a healthy balance between an individual's work and personal life to minimize the potential for leaders to become isolated and out of touch. Time to cultivate family relationships and outside interests is essential if the executive is to view his or her success as personally meaningful.
- **Build personality and related assessments** into the organization's managerial selection and succession planning processes. New research has suggested that measurements to determine a person's propensity to morally disengage (e.g.,

when they rationalize or blame others for their own unethical choices) can help predict who is more likely to engage in unethical or harmful behavior (Rockwood, 2020). These assessments are relatively inexpensive and easy to administer.

- **Work with trained employee assistance and other professionals** to diagnose psychological disorders. This can help organizational leadership develop more self-awareness and insight about how to overcome personal limitations.
- **Stress the ethical climate of the organization during the on-boarding process** so that new employees enter the organization with a clear understanding of the organization's expectations about ethical compliance—before any negative behaviors have a chance to develop.

Organizational Transparency

Organizational strategies designed to increase accountability and minimize opportunities for unchecked risk-taking include:

- **Implement and enforce a code of business conduct** that comprehensively defines organizational expectations, and work to continuously increase awareness of and compliance with these standards through training and periodic internal communications.
- **Develop an ethical culture that empowers people** in the organization to speak up and air their dissenting opinions. This type of environment will help to keep leaders grounded in reality and ensure that a thorough review of alternatives takes place for all key issues.
- **Ensure that the company's governance system is truly independent** and made up of board members who will not hesitate to ask questions, get involved, and challenge the organization's leadership as and when appropriate.
- **Set up internal checks and balances** such as regular audits of critical processes and resources that will quickly surface potential issues. High-level reporting of the audit findings can serve as a prudent check and balance on the use of power and authority by senior executives.
- **Establish an office of the ombudsman and/or a 1–800 ethics hotline** to encourage employees to confidentially speak out about unethical actions and decisions that may be occurring within the organization.

Conclusions

It would be a mistake to assume that it is only individuals who are morally corrupt or unprincipled who fall victim to ethical violations or become toxic leaders. To the contrary, the paradox of success is that it is the people who are the most ethical and successful that tend to inexplicably self-destruct at the very peak of their career.

The intersection of success and the potential for risky actions by leaders is clearly a dangerous crossroad. Extreme personal autonomy at work—coupled with the likely egotism and arrogance that comes from a history of success—sets up a potentially disastrous dynamic. Despite a history of success and a rock-solid reputation, it is important for leaders to understand that they can quickly lose it all if they give in to the inevitable temptations waiting for them at the top of most organizations.

Ensuring the implementation of the guardrails outlined in this chapter, along with additional institutional changes that we will discuss in a later chapter, may not shield leaders from every possible risk, but they can provide some meaningful protections along the way. If your efforts can keep even one executive from flaming out and destroying their life and career (and potentially your organization's reputation in the process), that will have been a good day's work.

References

Austen, B. (2012, August). Do you *really* want to be like Steve Jobs? *Wired*.

Berglas, S. (1986). *The success syndrome: Hitting bottom when you reach the top*. Plenum Press.

Blotnick, S. (1987). *Ambitious men: Their drives, dreams, and delusions*. Viking.

Boddy, C.R. (2011). The corporate psychopath theory of the global financial crisis. *Journal of Business Ethics (102)*, 255–259. doi: 10.1007/s10551-011-0810-4.

Ciulla, J. B. (2004). Ethics and leadership effectiveness. In J. Antonakis, A. T. Cianciolo, & R. J. Sternberg (Eds.), *The nature of leadership* (pp. 302–327). Sage.

Ciulla, J. B. (1998). *Ethics: The heart of leadership*. Praeger.

Collins, J. (2009). *How the mighty fall*. Collins Business Essentials.

Conger, J. (1990). The dark side of leadership. *Organizational Dynamics, 19*, 44–55.

Greycourt (2008). *The financial crisis and the collapse of ethical behavior*. Greycourt & Co. Whitepaper No. 44. https://icma.org/documents/financial-crisis-and-collapse-ethical-behavior-white-paper.

Kelly, C. M. (1988). *The destructive achiever*. Addison-Wesley.

Kets de Vries, M. F. (1989). Leaders who self-destruct: the causes and cures. *Organizational Dynamics*, 5–17.

LaBier, D. (1986). *Modern madness: The emotional fallout of success*. Addison-Wesley.

Ludwig, D. C., & Longenecker, C. O. (1993). The "Bathsheba syndrome": The ethical failure of successful leaders. *Journal of Business Ethics*, 12, 265–273.

Maccoby, M. (2003). *The productive narcissist: the promise and peril of visionary leadership*. Broadway Books.

McIntosh, G. L., & Rima, S. D. (1997). *Overcoming the dark side of leadership: The paradox of personal dysfunction*. Baker Books.

Moore, C., Detert, J. R., Klebe Trevino, L., Baker, V.L. and Mayer, D.M. (2012). Why employees do bad things: Moral disengagement and unethical organizational behavior. *Personnel Psychology, 65*: 1–48.

Nielsen, R. P. (1987). What can managers do about unethical management? *Journal of Business Ethics, 4*, 65–70.

Price, T. L. (2000). Explaining ethical failures of leadership. *The Leadership & Organization Development Journal 12*, 177–184.

Price, T. L. (2006). *Understanding ethical failures in leadership*. Cambridge University Press.

Rockwood, K. (2020). Assessing personalities. *SHRM*. https://www.shrm.org/hr-today/news/all-things-work/pages/personality-assessments.aspx.

Sullivan, B. & Olson, E. (2023, April 5). 5 things to know about Donald Trump's felony charges. *NPR*. https://www.npr.org/2023/04/04/1168094097/donald-trump-felony-charges-reaction-trial.
VanKleef, M. Homan, G.A., Finkenauer, A.C., Gundemir, S., & Stamkon, E. (2011). Breaking the rules to rise to power: How norm violators gain power in the eyes of others. *Social Psychological and Personality Science*, *2*(5), 500–507.
Wikipedia (n.d.). *Indictment of Donald Trump*. https://en.wikipedia.org/wiki/Indictment_of_Donald_Trump.

Suggested Additional Reading

Culbert, S.A. (2017). *Good people, bad managers: How work culture corrupts good intentions*. Oxford University Press.
George, B. (2007). *True north: Discover your authentic leadership*. Jossey-Bass.
Rath, T. & Conchie, B. (2008). *Strengths based leadership: Great leaders, teams, and why people follow*. Gallup Press.
Sutton, R. (2007). *The no asshole rule: Building a civilized workplace and surviving one that isn't*. Warner Business Books.

HR's Role in the Management of Organizational Culture and Employee Well-Being

Chapter 8
The Critical Organizational Role of HR Practitioners

HR serves as a "serious buffer" for other employees in the organization—between management and employees. We are the "organizational shock absorbers." If HR professionals won't stand up to a bad manager, who will? But HR pays a heavy price for doing that. (Daniel, 2012)

HR professionals are in a unique position to help create the checks and balances necessary to mitigate the organizational impact of toxic leaders. In this chapter we will examine the varied roles of HR practitioners in responding to and preventing—or at least minimizing—the organizational toxicity caused by abusive leaders, the complexities of managing these various responsibilities, and what organizations tend to expect from them.

Organizational Roles of HR Professionals

A review of the relevant management and practitioner literature suggests that HR professionals have at least five unique organizational roles when it comes to their protection of employees from toxic leaders and the organizational toxicity caused by abuse or mistreatment (e.g., harassment, discrimination, workplace bullying, and the like). These include corporate insider with primary responsibility for helping to manage interpersonal conflicts, employee advocate, protector of management interests, personal target of management abuse, and toxin handler. Each of these roles will be examined next.

Role as Corporate Insider with Responsibility to Help Manage Interpersonal Conflicts

HR professionals are integral actors in situations of interpersonal dispute and are widely viewed as the organizational insiders best suited to take a leading role in the prevention and elimination of abusive misconduct at work (Daniel & Metcalf, 2016). HR tends to be a reflection and extension of the management philosophy and practices of the organization's top leaders (Yamada, 2009). If senior leaders do not condemn bad behavior, the message to their organization is that they are actually condoning it. Their silence speaks volumes to employees about what really matters (getting results at any cost), and what does not (respect, civility, and kindness). HR simply cannot do the important job of preventing or minimizing toxicity without full support from the organization's senior leaders.

https://doi.org/10.1515/9783111201771-008

Role as Employee Advocate

Another key role for HR professionals is to serve as an employee advocate to protect employees from discrimination, abuse, or mistreatment at work (Society for Human Resource Management, 2016). This requires taking action to protect employees from abusive managers, while at the same time safeguarding the prerogative of managers to push employees to meet (or exceed) company performance goals even though they may be perceived as a "tough boss" (Daniel, 2009).

Striking that balance, though, is not an easy task due in large part to conflicts among multiple and competing HR roles; a lack of specific organizational policies and guidelines for dealing with misconduct; and ambiguous definitions and criteria for determining when behavior rises to the level of abuse (Fox & Cowan, 2015).

Role as Protector of Management and Organizational Interests

Senior leaders in a study by Daniel (2013) suggested that HR practitioners possess considerable strength in four key areas that serve to benefit and protect the interests of both management and the organization: education and training of the workforce; mitigation of risk to the organization (e.g., minimizing the potential for lawsuits or regulatory violations); providing reliable basic HR services (e.g., policy development, strategies about human capital deployment, hiring, benefits, and communication); and protecting the interests of both employees and management (e.g., investigating and resolving workplace conflicts, coaching and challenging senior leaders about important people-related decisions).

In partnership with the company's legal counsel, HR is called upon to investigate employee complaints of the abusive treatment of employees. If the allegations of misconduct are confirmed, HR generally first confers with legal counsel and then with senior leaders to determine the appropriate consequences (Daniel, 2013). The investigative aspect of the role has often caused HR to be perceived as the "internal police" of the organization, a characterization to which most practitioners object and a role which they generally find to be uncomfortable (Fox & Cowan, 2015).

There is a paradox inherent in the multiple roles that HR must navigate, especially when it comes to representing the interests of both the employee and the organization. Ulrich (1997) argues that HR professionals "can both represent employee needs *and* implement management agendas, be the voice of the employee *and* the voice of management, act as partner to both employees *and* managers" (p. 45)—but it clearly is not easy to straddle these often competing roles (Grillo, 2014).

It is not surprising, then, that more than half of the HR leaders responding to a survey by a global talent management firm about the complexity of the HR role reported feeling "overwhelmed" and 52 percent reported that they "did not have the ability to fully cope" with it (Society for Human Resource Management, 2013).

Unfortunately, HR is often perceived by employees as siding with management in some of the worst workplace bullying situations brought to their attention. There is all too often some truth to support that perception. The uncomfortable dilemma commonly faced by HR practitioners is aptly stated by Yamada (2013):

> In good and bad workplaces alike, ***HR answers to top management,*** not to individual employees. Too many well-meaning team players have learned that lesson painfully, thinking that a seemingly empathetic HR manager is a sort of confidante or counselor. There are plenty of good, supportive HR people out there, but ultimately their job is to support the employer's hiring and personnel practices and interests.

Role as the Personal Target of Management Abuse

It may be somewhat surprising to learn that HR professionals are sometimes "caught in the crossfire" too. Recent studies suggest that between 27 percent (Daniel, 2012) and 31.4 percent (Society for Human Resource Management, 2012) of HR practitioners have personally been the targets of abusive mistreatment at work. Interestingly, most of the abuse is generated toward HR by members of the organization's senior leadership or by their immediate supervisor (Society for Human Resource Management, 2012). There can be no doubt that personally being a target of abuse and mistreatment makes it exponentially harder (if not actually impossible) for HR to protect other employees in the organization.

How do HR professionals make sense of this abusive mistreatment? In a study conducted by Daniel (2012), HR practitioners suggested that it is the nature of the organizational role of HR itself that may substantially contribute to the dynamic. Why might this be? HR practitioners are frequently required to coach or challenge business leaders in order to achieve the best decisions possible for the organization. At times, these discussions can get quite intense, triggering a negative or defensive response that subsequently results in backlash or retribution in the form of bullying and other negative tactics toward the HR professional.

Role as "Organizational Toxin Handler"

Layoffs, harassment, discrimination, mergers and acquisitions, personality conflicts, or an abusive boss are just a few of the many types of workplace situations that can generate intense emotional pain for employees—feelings like anger, frustration, stress, disappointment, and anxiety. If these types of situations are managed poorly, the chronic anger or prolonged stress these situations create results in an undesirable byproduct known as *organizational toxicity.*

Most of these workplace events are fairly predictable—even somewhat inevitable. It is the way organizations handle them (or do not) that can create a serious problem for employees and, ultimately, the organizations that they serve (Kulik, Creegan, Metz, & Brown, 2009).

HR practitioners are regularly confronted by distressed employees who bring these types of emotionally charged problems to them based on their desire to ensure that the issues are properly addressed (Kulik, Creegan, Metz, & Brown, 2009). In responding to these situations, HR practitioners serve their organizations as *"toxin handlers"*—defined as empathetic managers who are willing to try to address the pain, suffering, and emotional turmoil often experienced by employees at work (Daniel, 2020, 2018).

Others have used the term *"emotional laborers"* to describe the role HR plays in resolving conflict situations (Fox & Cowan, 2015). Similarly, it has also been suggested by HR practitioners that they serve as *"organizational shock absorbers"* given their frequent involvement with the emotional stress and tension caused by the abusive leader in their efforts to resolve the situation (Daniel, 2012).

In a recent study, 58% of HR practitioners said that they help employees deal with toxic emotions daily—you heard that right, **daily**! (Daniel, 2018). That suggests that this role, though not widely understood until now, is a significant one in terms of the actual work that we do.

Practitioners feel that the toxin-handling work is disproportionately assumed by HR practitioners, and three-quarters (73.1%) felt that this work was not recognized or appreciated by senior leaders in their organizations. Why? They surmised that it was largely invisible due to the expectation that HR will maintain confidentiality and privacy for employees who seek their help. Another study reported that, "almost 25% of their time [referring to HR], on average, is spent on emotionally charged problems" (Falcone, 2002).

For all these reasons and more, when it comes to dealing with toxic leaders and organizational toxicity, there is perhaps no HR function that is more important to employees and the organization than serving as a "toxin handler". When performing this work, HR engages in six core activities: empathetic listening, suggesting solutions and providing resources, working behind the scenes and providing a safe space, strategically communicating and reframing difficult messages, as well as advising and coaching managers (Daniel, 2018; Daniel, 2020).

By helping employees manage difficult workplace decisions and situations, HR enables other employees to stay focused and do their jobs. Without them, the organizational toxicity would continue to build, resulting in higher levels of turnover, increased health costs, more litigation, and reduced levels of employee morale, productivity, and profitability (Society for Human Management, 2019; Society for Human Resource Management, 2016).

As aptly noted by several study participants (Daniel, 2018):

> if you do not have that person who can sit down with people and be compassionate, be a good listener, be a good communicator, I think problems fester, they escalate, and you have huge problems in the end. So, if organizations do have people who are capable of being the toxic handlers, you're going to have a more efficient operation. You're going to have an operation who handles

problems at a lower level and they never get out of control. So, I think it [having a toxin handler] has a huge impact on an organization.

I've had this said to me by the executives I work with that they think that the support that I give them enables them to do their jobs and to be successful in their roles. Therefore, it drives the success of the business.

In addition, because the toxin handler helps to de-escalate emotional situations and make employees feel valued in the process, their work also helps to reduce the potential for lawsuits and claims of discrimination and harassment. There is no doubt that the work of an organizational toxin handler is immensely valuable and important to both employees and to their organizations. Given this, it remains somewhat paradoxical that this work is so often undervalued and somewhat invisible inside most organizations.

Conclusions

Creating and sustaining a psychologically healthy workplace—built on mutual respect for all—benefits both employees *and* their organizations. The empirical evidence unequivocally confirms that a respectful workplace environment results in higher levels of employee morale and job satisfaction, lower turnover, reduced health costs, higher productivity, and greater profitability for the organization. Coincidentally, demonstrating the courage and leadership necessary to confront toxic and destructive leaders is likely to result in a more effective and admired HR department too.

References

Daniel, T.A. (2009). *"Tough boss" or workplace bully: A grounded theory study of insights from human resource professionals*. Doctoral Dissertation. http://search.proquest.com/docview/305169091.

Daniel, T.A. (2012). Caught in the crossfire: When HR practitioners become targets of bullying. *Employment Relations Today, 39*(1), 9–16. http://onlinelibrary.wiley.com/doi/10.1002/ert.21349/abstract.

Daniel, T.A. (2013, Summer). Executive perceptions about the effectiveness of human resources. *Employment Relations Today, 40*(2), 1–11. http://onlinelibrary.wiley.com/doi/10.1002/ert.21405/abstract.

Daniel, T.A. & Metcalf, G.S. (2016). *Stop bullying at work: Strategies and tools for HR, legal & risk management professionals* (2nd edition). SHRM Books.

Daniel, T.A. (2018). *Managing toxic emotions at work: An empirical study of HR's role and its Impact on personal well-being and organizational effectiveness*. doi: 10.13140/RG.2.2.16315.26408.

Daniel, T.A. (2020). *Organizational toxin handlers: The critical role of HR, OD, & coaching practitioners in managing toxic workplace situations*. Palgrave Macmillan.

Falcone, P. (2002, October). Understanding the HR mind-set. *HR Magazine, 47*(10), 117–122.

Fox, S. & Cowan, R. L. (2015, February). Being pushed and pulled: A model of U.S. HR professionals' roles in bullying situations. *Personnel Review, 44*(1), 119–139.

Fox, S. & Cowan, R. L. (2015, January). Revision of the workplace bullying checklist: The importance of human resource management's role in defining and addressing workplace bullying. *Human Resource Management Journal, 25*(1), 116–130.

Grillo, M.C. (2014, October 8). *Straddling the line or embracing the dichotomy: HR's role as an employee advocate as necessary to remain (or become) a business partner.* http://www.cornellhrreview.org/straddling-the-line-or-embracing-the-dichotomy-hrs-role-as-an-employee-advocate-as-necessary-to-remaining-or-becoming-a-business-partner/.

Kulik, C.T., Creegan, C. Metz, I. & M. Brown (2009, September/October). HR managers as toxic handlers: The buffering effect of formalizing toxic handling. *Human Resource Management, 48*(5), 695–716, footnote 21.

Meisinger, S.R. (2005). The four Cs of the HR profession: Being competent, curious, courageous, and caring about people. *Human Resource Management, 44*(2), 189–194.

Society for Human Resource Management (2012, February 28). *SHRM survey findings: Workplace bullying.* http://www.shrm.org/research/surveyfindings/articles/pages/workplacebullying.aspx.

Society for Human Resource Management (2013, August 2). *Organizational complexity overwhelms many HR leaders.* https://www.shrm.org/hrdisciplines/orgempdev/articles/pages/organizational-complexity-overwhelms-hr.aspx.

Society for Human Resource Management (2016). *Employee satisfaction and engagement: Revitalizing a changing workforce.* https://www.shrm.org/Research/SurveyFindings/Articles/Documents/2016-Employee-Job-Satisfaction-and-Engagement-Report.pdf.

Society for Human Resource Management Foundation (2016). *Creating a more human workplace where employees and businesses thrive.* https://www.shrm.org/about/foundation/products/documents/4-16%20human%20workplace-final.pdf.

Society for Human Resource Management (2016). *The SHRM body of competency and knowledge.* https://www.shrm.org/Documents/SHRM-BoCK-FINAL.pdf.

Society for Human Resource Management (2019). *The high cost of a toxic workplace culture: How culture impacts the workforce—and the bottom line.* https://pages.shrm.org/2019culturereport?_ga=2.46299751.1379352704.1569245079-1873814319.1519658911.

Ulrich, D. (1997). *HR champions: The next agenda for adding value and delivering results.* HBR Press.

Yamada, D. (2009, January 4). HR was useless. *New Workplace Institute Blog.* https://newworkplace.wordpress.com/2009/01/04/hr-was-useless/.

Yamada, D. (2013, October 28). HR, workplace bullying, and the abandoned target. New Workplace Institute Blog. https://newworkplace.wordpress.com/2013/10/28/hr-workplace-bullying-and-the-abandoned-target/.

Chapter 9
Strategies to Help Employees Cope With Difficult Bosses

If you were ever in doubt, it should now be clear that bad bosses are everywhere. SHRM's recent research demonstrated that they have driven 20% of U.S. employees out of their jobs in the past five years alone—at a turnover cost greater than $223 billion! (Society for Human Resource Management, 2019). Yes, you read that right. Toxic work cultures drive away a staggering 1 in 5 employees which comes with an annual $44.6 billion-dollar cost to American organizations.

The Compelling Case for Quitting

Given the prevalence and the cost associated with bad bosses, U.S. corporations clearly have a problem. These statistics mean that many employees are in jobs that they don't like or in situations where they live in fear of their boss.

People stay in jobs or continue to work with bosses they don't like for many reasons. Some have been brow-beaten for so long that they have lost the energy to even look for a new job and now feel hopelessly stuck. Others believe in their organization's mission, feel that their work is meaningful, or both. Some individuals really like their colleagues who they have worked with for so long that they feel like family. Still others stay because they need the income or the job pays too well for them to leave and find a comparable position.

These explanations are all valid reasons not to make a change. But it is important to remember that sometimes the best possible decision under the circumstances may simply be to leave a toxic situation altogether, despite the loss of salary, status, stability, seniority, social connections, and other benefits that have been accumulated over the years.

We humans are psychologically hard-wired to be "loss averse". What I mean by that is that we are generally reluctant to give up on something we have invested so much to build—our professional livelihood in this case. Although staying may seem more secure than leaving, it actually comes with many risks.

A Swedish study of more than 3,100 men over a 10-year period found that employees who had a toxic manager (which the study defined as incompetent, inconsiderate, secretive, and uncommunicative) were 60% more likely to suffer a heart attack or other life-threatening cardiac condition. The less competent the study participants rated the leadership skills of their boss, the higher their risk for heart disease (Nyberg, Alfredsson, Theorell, Westerlund, Vahtera, & Kivimaki, 2009).

https://doi.org/10.1515/9783111201771-009

This was one of the earliest studies to demonstrate a "dose-response" relationship between concrete managerial behaviors and objectively assessed ischemic heart disease among employees. Translation: the longer you work for a toxic boss, the higher your risk of being hospitalized for a serious health issue or having a fatal heart attack.

Other studies in American workplaces have shown that people with toxic bosses are more susceptible to chronic stress, depression, and anxiety, all of which increase the risk of a lowered immune system, colds, and strokes, in addition to heart attacks (Abbajay, 2018).

While the idea of quitting may seem scary, the reality of staying for too long in a job with a toxic boss is actually even more terrifying given the potentially significant impact to your own personal health and well-being. Your professional future may depend on your early decision to leave as well. There is a voluminous body of research confirming that toxic bosses almost never change their behavior and that there is commonly a significant and deleterious impact on the target's self-confidence, overall sense of well-being, as well as on their physical and mental health status (Workplace Bullying Institute, 2021).

For all of these reasons, the consequences of staying in a bad situation must be carefully considered when weighing possible options. Generally, the best strategy is to leave a bad situation—sooner rather than later—if this is a viable decision.

Alternative Individual Response Strategies

For many affected employees, though, leaving is simply not a viable option. If that is the case, there are numerous potential practical responses that might be deployed, either individually or in combination. According to Shufelt and Longenecker (2017), these include:
- Put yourself in your boss's shoes;
- Get on the same page as your boss;
- Work hard to know and understand your boss's strengths and weaknesses;
- Conduct regular assessments of the overall quality of your current relationship with your boss and conduct an annual strengths, weaknesses, opportunities and threats analysis;
- Communicate using your boss's rules (e.g., if he uses text and never calls on the phone, follow his lead);
- Be proactive and stay aligned with your boss;
- Establish your "brand" and make it a practice to under-promise and over-deliver;
- Be a problem solver;
- Always show respect for your boss (even if he or she might not deserve it); and
- Know when it's time to leave the situation behind.

In addition to possibly mitigating the impact of a toxic leader, these are also good general strategies for building your professional career and for improving your work relationships. Upon first glance, these suggestions may seem rather trite, but it is a truism that we sometimes tend to overlook the most straightforward and easy solutions close at hand.

Evidence-Based Strategies for Individuals

There are several promising strategies to reduce the damage caused by working for a toxic leader. They are recommended by numerous HR practitioners who have personally lived through—and survived—such a situation (Daniel, 2012). In the words of those study participants, all of whom were active HR practitioners, some of the most promising approaches suggested by individuals who have been on the receiving end of a toxic boss include:

— **Just "wait it out" knowing that the individual will soon be promoted or transferred**
So, a lot of people are like, "Okay, if I keep my head down and get through this year and a half to two years, I'm going to have a new boss and then everything's going to be all gravy again. I think a lot of people accept it [toxic leadership] because of that."
You can say [to yourself], "Hey, look, I can outlast this guy . . . he only has this much longer. It will pass."

— **Use the chain of command to report abuse**
*The only avenue that I really know of is the chain of command . . . it depends on where you are. But if the toxicity is coming **from** the chain of command, it's kind of hard to go complain to the chain of command, though.*

— **Avoid the toxic leader**
You just avoid . . . and you try to stay out of his path and don't even walk past his office.
If you can understand what their motivations are then you can accomplish what they're looking to do and essentially stay off their radar.

— **Identify a person the toxic leader trusts and work through that individual**
Your best bet might be to go around them. What I would personally try and do would be to look at who their network is, who are their peers, who do they trust, and maybe work through them.

- **Make it a point to learn what not to do from the toxic leader**

[After working with a toxic leader] I can say, "Hey, those are absolutely no's for me" so I will make sure I don't do those things.

I believe that you learn from that situation and learn what not to do. And you take those lessons learned and you apply them to your future roles, positions, and then that way, you help protect individuals and learn and build that cohesive, well-organized unit.

- **Communicate regularly and provide feedback intended to help the toxic leader become more self-aware of his impact on others**

. . . you try to make them aware of the impact of their actions.

- **Check policies, procedures, laws, and regulations to see if his actions are improper or illegal and approach the problem from that angle**

The first thing I would do is to make sure that whatever activity they're doing is in violation of some sort of [policy or] regulation and make sure they are aware of that. If the behavior continued, then I would feel compelled to go to their supervisor.

- **Provide "cover" for subordinates in order to protect them**

What I tried to do is shield my [people] from any of it. They know that I'm going to try to step up and be the buffer—the one who is going to take that "face shot", for lack of better terms.

. . . you see the toll it's taking on your people and you say, "If I am not here as a buffer, it's going to be that much worse for them", so you say to yourself, "Can I take it? Can I take it more? Yeah, I can take it more." And then people say, "Thank you for not leaving. We know you could have."

- **Teach subordinates what "good leadership" looks like and regularly practice it so that toxic behaviors are not imitated**

Great leaders really take the time to show you what right looks like.

- **File a formal organizational complaint**

Although filing an official organizational complaint was noted as a possible option, it was not viewed as one likely to actually resolve the problem. In fact, some suggested that going to HR or a senior leader could actually even wind up making the situation worse.

Some Final Thoughts

There is no one right way to respond to a toxic leader or a toxic situation because each circumstance poses its own unique set of challenges. However, hopefully these recommendations will provide some ideas about how you might counsel an employee currently in a difficult situation, or how you might directly respond to a toxic leader if their abuse is being directed at you (and I desperately hope for your sake that this is never the case).

If leaving a toxic situation is a viable option, it is (sadly) probably the best response given the dire potential health consequences that end up hurting far too many. I simply cannot emphasize enough how important it is for the target of the abuse to make that decision early—before irreparable damage occurs to one's personal health and well-being and before one's confidence is so shattered that it makes it nearly impossible to recover from the situation and search for a new—and likely better—opportunity.

References

Abbajay, M. (2018, September 7). What to do when you have a bad boss. *Harvard Business Review*. https://hbr.org/2018/09/what-to-do-when-you-have-a-bad-boss.

Daniel, T.A. (2012, Spring). Caught in the crossfire: When HR practitioners become targets of bullying. *Employment Relations Today Journal, 39*(1), 9–16.

Nyberg, A., Alfredsson, L, Theorell, T., Westerlund, H., Vahtera, J. & M. Kivimaki (2009). Managerial leadership and ischaemic heart disease among employees: The Swedish WOLF study. *Journal of Occupational and Environmental Medicine, 66*(1), 51–55.

Shufelt, J.W., Jr. & Longenecker, C.O. (2017, November). Practical lessons learned for dealing with toxic leaders and bad bosses. *Military Review Online Exclusive*. http://www.armyupress.army.mil/Journals/Military-Review/Online-Exclusive/2017-Online-Exclusive-Articles/Practical-Lessons/.

Society for Human Resource Management (2019). *The high cost of a toxic workplace culture: How culture impacts the workforce—and the bottom line*. https://pages.shrm.org/2019culturereport?_ga=2.46299751.1379352704.1569245079-1873814319.1519658911.

Workplace Bullying Institute (2021). *The WBI 2021 U.S. Workplace Bullying Study*. https://workplacebullying.org/2021-wbi-survey/.

Chapter 10
The Performance-Conduct Circle: Helping Employees Understand That Results Are Just Part of the Equation

We have now thoroughly examined the data and it is unequivocal: despite their ability to generate results, toxic leaders invariably hurt their organizations—almost always leaving them in far worse shape than when they started. Employees often describe workplace cultures where toxic leaders thrive as disrespectful, non-inclusive, unethical, cut-throat, or abusive—not exactly suggestive of an environment where employees can flourish and feel safe.

In fact, the impact to the physical and mental health of employees from a toxic workplace is so severe that it has led the U.S. Surgeon General to issue a call to action to employers to take immediate steps to eliminate abusive and cut-throat workplaces. The 2022 report outlines a series of five essential areas of focus to ensure employee mental health and well-being. These include protection from harm, connection and community, work-life harmony, mattering at work, and opportunity for growth (U.S. Surgeon General, 2022). I encourage you to take some time to read the report as it is comprehensive and contains many good suggestions.

If the consequences of their destructive behavior are so bad, a reasonable question to ask (yet again) is this: how is it that toxic leaders continue to get promoted and/or remain in positions of leadership? Simply put, *they get results*. However, organizations have a moral obligation to take proactive steps to create the conditions for physical and psychological safety at work to ensure both the productivity and emotional well-being of their employees. They can do this by paying attention not just *what* an individual achieves, but also to *how* those results are accomplished (including the negative impact to employee health and well-being) in order to achieve optimum organizational functioning and success.

Many organizations suffer from "rebel" high performers—senior leaders and even family members of the owner who consistently get stellar results but act in a way that negatively impacts their subordinates and colleagues, along with their organization. They operate as if they are "special" and seem to assume that everyone else thinks so too. They are individuals who operate as if their high performance gives them license to operate with impunity and as if they can do no wrong.

Their logic typically follows a path like this: "I generate the most revenue in this division, so they can't touch me." It likewise might sound like this: "I've been here for 30 years and I get results—this is just who I am . . . so deal with it." You undoubtedly know one or more of these types of people.

The question then becomes: how do you get these "toxic stars" back on track so that they can continue to get results but not burn your organization down in the pro-

https://doi.org/10.1515/9783111201771-010

cess? The key lies in holding them accountable in a way that appeals to their career interests and doesn't make you the bad guy. In this chapter, we will consider a practical way to deal with a toxic leader before they have wrecked their career or negatively impacted the well-being of your employees and/or the organization's culture.

The Performance-Conduct Circle

Many super successful individuals fail to understand that they are responsible for both their performance (aka their actual results) *and* their conduct (the way they go about getting those results). Think about it as a performance-conduct circle: the top half is their performance and results and the bottom half is their behavior and its impact on others. Both components are mission critical to the creation of a positive workplace culture—results and process.

The problem is that top performers typically believe that their results are all that matter. When their bad behavior drives employees to leave the organization, the organization is weakened and the employees who remain are left feeling demoralized and unmotivated.

Sometimes it helps to have a "script" to follow to get ideas about the type of conversation that you want to have or that might be the most effective. A possible solution: meet with the individual in a confidential setting, one-on-one. Explain that you want to hold a career and executive coaching discussion about their longer-term career goals and then share some ideas about how they can be even more successful going forward.

According to a brilliant—yet deceptively simple—strategy initially outlined by Falcone (2022), at that point, you can draw a circle on a piece of paper or on a whiteboard and place a line through the middle, cutting the circle in half. Write the word "Performance" in the top half of the circle and "Conduct" in the bottom half of the circle. Explain that the employee, like everyone else, is responsible for both halves. Your conversation might sound like this:

> Rob, all of us—me included—are responsible for both our performance as well as our behavior. It's two halves of the same whole. In the top half of the circle, you're knocking it out of the park. You are consistently a top salesperson in our division. I think that's pretty impressive and our senior leadership thinks so too.
>
> But here's the thing: you are also responsible for the bottom half of the circle—your conduct and behavior. That includes creating a friendly and inclusive work environment where others feel comfortable seeking out your counsel and where you serve as a mentor and role model for other employees. That's where you're not meeting expectations, in my opinion.
>
> How do you feel you're performing in terms of the conduct portion of the circle right now?

Some interesting dialogue may ensue at this point, so simply listen to the individual's self-assessment and level of personal awareness before responding.

Increasing Self-Awareness

The conversation might continue like this:

> Rob, I hear what you're saying, but allow me to share what things look like from my vantage point. I sometimes see you appearing to diminish others, making remarks about their lack of productivity, or saying that they are leaving you with all the 'heavy lifting' to meet sales goals. Can you recall ever making comments along those lines?

> ("Yes, but . . . ")

> OK, there's no need to justify anything. I'm just trying to raise your awareness. But here's the catch: I have to hold you accountable for your own perception management just like I do my own and every other member of this division. There have been numerous reports from others that you are often disrespectful; frankly, the term 'asshole' has come up quite a few times to describe your interactions with others. What do you think you could do to help the situation and be seen as more of a team player?

Note the use of phrases like "sometimes" or "from time to time." You're much better off using that kind of limited language than by employing extreme adverbs like "always" and "never," which often are exaggerated, frustrate the recipient of your message and trigger defensiveness.

Longer-Term Career Appeal

You then have an opportunity to move into the closing of your argument:

> If you can become as strong in the bottom half of the circle (conduct) as you are in the top half (performance), then the sky's your limit. Yes, you're the top salesperson in the division, but that is not going to be enough to go to the next level. You also have to be able to build strong teams, coach and mentor subordinates, and build a great reputation as an ethical leader and communicator.

> In short, what got you here won't get you there. As you progress through your career, you can succeed best and quickest by helping others to succeed. Your success is measured **through** people, not **despite** them. Further developing your skills in the areas of leadership, communication and team- building prepare you to take on greater responsibilities with bigger teams in larger leagues.

> I'd like to be the one to help you get there. I want to be the career mentor and coach to make it safe for you to learn how to do this the right way—right here and now—while I'm here to have your back. I'd like to be your sponsor and mentor, but it's going to take a significant turnaround in terms of how you've been approaching others.

> Are you up for the challenge? Are you ready to reinvent yourself? I'd like you to give that some thought and come back to me sometime during the coming week so we can discuss this further.

Appealing to a top performer's career interests and personal growth strategy is likely to yield the greatest results. Once the recipient of your message can funnel your communication through his or her personal interests, the potential for the individual to accept and internalize your message skyrockets.

Legal Implications

In addition to the potential to improve the individual's self-awareness, there is a legal motivation to this approach as well. You will have developed a strong record in terms of identifying the issue and suggesting to the employee that is it imperative for their future success to change their problematic and toxic behavior: if you move later to progressive disciplinary action, you can document the date and time of this meeting as your initial attempt at notifying the individual of the problematic conduct.

Know that it will always be a challenge to gain buy-in when trying to convince top performers to change their approach with respect to peer or subordinate communications. Why? Because they think that they know it all; otherwise, how else could they get such amazing results, year after year after year??

Despite the challenges involved in dealing with a toxic star, addressing the issue head-on is the right thing to do for employee morale, for the toxic star's future success, and for the organization as a whole. Maximize the chances of engagement and turnaround by convincing them that you can help them scale their career progression and financial achievements according to their own self-interests.

Bottom line, though: if a toxic leader cannot or will not change, the sad truth is that the best option is to hold them accountable for their abusive way of operating and fairly quickly show them the door. Regardless of their ability to deliver results, toxic leaders are, in the end, simply too expensive to keep.

References

Falcone, P. (2022, July 28). *Viewpoint: Why Stellar Performance Should Not Justify Toxic Behavior*. https://www.shrm.org/resourcesandtools/hr-topics/employee-relations/pages/viewpoint-why-stellar-performance-should-not-justify-toxic-behavior.aspx.

U.S. Surgeon General (2022, October 22). *U.S. Surgeon General's Framework for Workplace Mental Health & Well-Being*. U.S. Department of Health and Human Services. https://www.hhs.gov/surgeongeneral/priorities/workplace-well-being/index.html.

Evidence-Based Strategies: Building Stronger Organizational Cultures

Chapter 11
Organizational Guardrails for Creating and Sustaining a Positive Workplace Climate

Organizational culture consists of a set of shared meanings, assumptions, values, and norms that guide the behavior of employees within an organization. It is created as a result of both explicit and implicit assumptions and understandings among employees and leaders—often described in its essence as *"the way we do things around here"* (Schein, 1992).

Developing a positive workplace climate involves building strong relationships between the organization and its and employees based on fairness, trust, and mutual respect. It takes time and energy to create this type of work environment, but it is well worth the time and effort. This type of culture leads to motivated, loyal, and high-performing employees who are focused on achieving the best results possible for their company.

Key Elements of a Positive Organizational Climate

Some of the key components in the creation of a positive organizational climate include the following:

- **Communication.** Ongoing, frequent two-way communication is one of the most important components of a comprehensive employee relations strategy. Interactive communication—both giving a message and actively listening to what is being said in response—builds trust between employees and their managers. Managers who use a combination of face-to-face, phone, and electronic communication are the most successful in engaging employees and building trusting relationships.
- **Trust.** Managers need to be alert and sensitive to the feelings of their employees. Exhibiting empathy and awareness is an important part of establishing a trusting relationship with employees. If employees do not trust their manager, the flow of upward communication will be compromised (or simply will not happen) and employees are not likely to do anything more at work then is absolutely required.

  Likewise, if managers do not trust the employees who work for them, the downward flow of communication will be negatively affected. You can demand compliance to organizational norms and values and you can require employees to perform their work, but commitment—built on mutual trust and respect— must be earned. When it exists, it confirms to employees that their manager really cares about them and creates the kind of organizational climate that allows great things to happen.

https://doi.org/10.1515/9783111201771-011

- **Ethics.** If a manager is not perceived by employees as having good business ethics, they will indirectly question the manager's motives (which may cause stress and have an impact on their overall performance).
- **Fairness.** All employees should be treated in a consistent manner under the same circumstances. This does not mean, however, that superior performance should not be singled out and rewarded.
- **Perceptions and Beliefs.** If employees believe the organization has fair policies and practices and tries to communicate truthfully, transparently, and sincerely, they will respond better than if they believe the organization is untrustworthy or is only telling part of the story. Frequent and honest communication will go a long way to ensure that employee beliefs and perceptions are related to the actual reality of the workplace.
- **Clear Expectations.** Employees need to know what to expect from their manager. No one likes to be surprised with new or conflicting requirements. Knowing what to expect reduces stress and helps employees focus on the job at hand, which is vital to achieve performance excellence.
- **Conflict Resolution.** Although conflicts arise in every organization, how they are handled varies widely. Dealing with issues head-on and resolving disputes fairly and quickly should be your company's ultimate goal.

As is the case with most strategies, there is no "one-size-fits-all" approach; instead, organizations should adopt the mission, vision, values, and strategies that fit their unique culture and operating needs. As HR practitioners, you will, undoubtedly, have a key role in these conversations and in helping to shape these decisions.

The Consequences of Inattention

If you and/or your management team mistakenly fail to prioritize employee relations as a key business issue, it is possible that the consequences may not be immediately felt. But make no mistake: there undoubtedly will be a negative impact on your organization at some point in the future. The only question is when that day of reckoning will occur—and how much it will cost your company.

Some of the potential consequences of a negative culture—one where employees feel disrespected and are frequently treated unfairly—include:
- **Unionization.** When employees perceive their workplace as unfair, they are more inclined to seek outside resources (such as a union) to help protect them and to negotiate issues on their behalf related to employment, benefits, and policies.
- **Employee Absenteeism.** Another major impact is a frequent increase in employee absenteeism. Unscheduled absences drive up the cost of doing business as a result of their impact on employee benefit costs, replacement workers, higher

stress levels among employees, additional training, and the decrease in overall employee performance.

– **Employee Turnover.** When employees do not trust their management and perceive that the company is not acting fairly, many will elect to leave the organization in search of work at a company where the situation is more positive. Employee turnover can significantly drive up costs as a result of the need to recruit for a replacement, training, and the anticipated reduction of performance results—both during the recruiting process and even during the period after the new hire begins on the job.

– **Increased Levels of Conflict**. In a toxic workplace climate, employees generally feel that the organization is unfair or does not care about them, or both. Such environments are characterized by escalating conflicts, bullying, harassment, increased workloads, and low levels of job satisfaction. As a result, the level of tension rises resulting in more interpersonal conflict.

– **Litigation.** If employees cannot resolve their disputes through fair systems offered internally, they will be increasingly likely to seek legal counsel and file a lawsuit. Defending a charge or lawsuit is costly—not only in terms of money (for attorney's fees and possibly settlement costs), but it can also eat up time and distract management from its primary focus on the business.

Evidence-Based Organizational Guardrails

In an earlier chapter, we discussed the factors that create a conducive environment for toxic leaders to flourish. We will now examine some of the "guardrails" that can be implemented to keep employees and leaders on the right path by building in "signs" and "guideposts", as well as policies and procedures, at some of the trickiest (and most dangerous) points individuals are likely to encounter along the way.

Four research-based strategies to help you build the scaffolding for a positive workplace culture will be discussed next. They include *prevention* strategies, *intervention* strategies, *restoration and recovery* strategies, and *accountability* strategies. Used in combination, these approaches will help to ensure that you have put controls in place to guard against the most likely challenges you are likely to face when it comes to toxic leaders taking actions that will weaken your culture or demoralize and drive away your employees.

Prevention Strategies

Based on a growing body of evidence-based research, some recommended strategies include:

– Develop a Culture of Respect, Appreciation, and Accountability

It is recommended that organizations take steps to move from a *culture of fear* to a *culture of respect, appreciation, and accountability* by establishing and maintaining a workplace culture that requires that both respect and dignity be afforded to all employees; that is, a workplace climate where employees feel valued, supported, where they are encouraged and accountable for doing their best work (Nowak & Zak, 2020).

In research released by the Society for Human Resource Management Foundation (2016), the respectful treatment of employees at all levels was found to be the single most important contributor to the overall job satisfaction. When employees perceive that their organization is fair, respectful, and committed to them, they tend to reciprocate by giving their best effort as well—a concept which has been referred to as *perceived organizational support* (Eisenberger, Huntington, Hutchison, & Sowa, 1986).

Moreover, there is research suggesting that organizations which create an ethical infrastructure to support a respectful culture (through the implementation of their policies, conflict management training, formal sanctions, transparency, communication, social norms, and conflict management climate, and accountability) are perceived as more successful in their interventions against the toxic tendencies of organizational leaders (Einarsen, Mykletun, Skogstad, Einarsen, & Salin, 2015).

– Well-Trained Leaders, Managers, and Supervisors

Supervisors and managers are the key link between employees and their company, and employees want (and expect) a lot from them; however, less than one-third of American workers report being engaged in their jobs in any given year. That low level of engagement is no fluke—it has been fairly consistent since 2000 when Gallup first began measuring and reporting on workplace engagement.

Gallup also found that the highest-performing managers and leaders possess a rare combination of five talents: they motivate their employees, assert themselves to overcome obstacles, create a culture of accountability, build trusting relationships, and make informed, unbiased decisions for the good of their team and company. There is a direct link between the improved performance of managers and leaders with respect to these "soft skills" in terms of employee engagement and company profitability (Gallup, 2015; Lombardo & McCall, 1984).

– Hire and Promote the Right People

A key strategy for avoiding future employee relations problems is to pay careful attention to your hiring and promotion process. Screen, select, and promote those individuals who possess empathy and compassion and who will contribute to a caring culture at work. Preventive measures include good interviewing skills and pre-employment screening (including a drug screen and background investigation that covers education, prior work history, any criminal background, plus a driver's license check).

While it is critically important to hire people with the right kind of experience and education, it is just as important to hire people who are a "good fit" for the organization—in terms of their communication style and general demeanor. The way a company operates (its "personality", if you will) can have a significant impact on whether a certain type of candidate will have a successful career at that particular organization. Hiring for "fit" should be a central part of the recruiting process.

Once hired, it is important to start employees off right by making sure they are familiar with the company's key policies and rules, organizational structure, chain-of-command, business philosophy, expectations, and company culture ("how we do things around here"). Companies typically offer "new hire training" within the first few weeks or months of employment to be sure that employees understand key issues from the start of the employment relationship. This is important so that employees do not inadvertently "cross a line" that they did not even know existed. And some companies even require employees to participate in this training even before they can begin their first full day in their assigned department.

In addition to this initial training, many companies match the new hire with a more seasoned employee who is the new employee's designated "mentor" for a specified time period (generally the first year of employment). The mentor is the new employee's "go-to" person in the company—it is with the mentor that the new employee can ask questions, understand how the politics and relationships work inside the company and generally learn their way around the organization. If the new hire is lucky, the mentor will become a friend and ally over the course of the mentor-mentee assignment.

– **Changes to the Promotion Process**
Examine Feedback from Multiple Levels. The promotion process is a strong leverage point. The promotional process should include an examination of feedback from multiple organizational levels. Failing to consider a variety of input may allow only a partial view of the person's leadership and potential for increasing assignments.

Given how politically savvy many toxic leaders tend to be, the boss is unlikely to be aware of their propensity to "kiss up and kick down". A focus on *how* results get accomplished creates a strong leverage point and may provide a more holistic picture of the individual and his readiness for additional responsibilities (or not).

> Our rating system promotes the end results instead of the ways and the means of how they [the toxic leader] get those results.

Examine Results of Employee Engagement and Satisfaction Surveys. The data collected from employee engagement and satisfaction surveys would provide valuable evidence about the leader's impact on his subordinates and should be considered during the promotion process.

Solicit Input from Former Senior Leaders. It may also be useful to contact former supervisors to ask for their input about the individual's capabilities and readiness for the particular assignment.

Regardless of how the promotional process is restructured, the overriding point is that it would be useful to expand the information available so that decision makers get a more holistic picture of the individual's strengths and weaknesses (and not just the limited—and often inaccurate—perception of his boss). Such a change to these processes would allow for more informed promotion and evaluation decisions and help to minimize the number of toxic leaders who progress within the system simply because their true character is unknown to their superiors.

– Implement Comprehensive Organizational Policies

Clear and unambiguous organizational policies can directly influence employee behavior. Why? Because they serve as formal announcements of the company's expectations on certain matters of importance. Policies also provide tools for managers and supervisors to use to react to violations of stated norms. Researchers and practitioners have recommended that organizational policies should be adopted or updated to include language that specifically details the type of abusive misconduct that is prohibited (along with examples). Such policies help to guide behavior and can be useful and effective as a deterrent to bad behavior.

Consider including a provision requiring *all* employees to notify management if they see a fellow employee being mistreated will ensure that co-workers who witness a problem feel duty bound to speak up and alert the company's management before the situation escalates further (American Bar Association, 2012). Given that policies and practices are considered to be contractually enforceable in most jurisdictions, it should be noted that HR typically works in close partnership with the company's legal counsel in order to navigate the myriad of potential issues with legal implications.

In my experience, the majority of litigation occurs when individuals feel that they were "not heard" or "not taken seriously". Instead, they feel that the company treated them unfairly and that they were not given a fair chance. You can avoid at least some of these problematic situations by implementing a system of progressive discipline. A clear and unambiguous disciplinary policy is critical to ensure that you have a fair process—one that protects employees from "knee-jerk" reactions by management while at the same time protecting your organization from employment-related lawsuits.

Generally, most progressive discipline policies include the following steps (and usually in the following order, but in exigent circumstances, termination might be the first and only action taken): verbal warning; written warning; suspension; and termination as the final step.

Chances are that your employees will view your system as fair and equitable if you have provided them with a fair chance to correct problematic behaviors before termination is invoked. This perception of fairness will help to minimize emotions and disruptions by other employees on those (hopefully) rare occasions when an employee must be terminated from employment.

– Engage in Reliable and Meaningful Communication

Consistent communication is connected with higher employee engagement, whether it occurs in person, over the phone, or electronically. HR can implement and enforce the company's conduct expectations through periodic training and frequent internal communications. It may also be pragmatic—as well as both cost- and time-effective—to incorporate conduct expectations into existing policies and programs rather than launching brand new initiatives from scratch (Daniel & Metcalf, 2016).

– Conduct Periodic Training about Conduct Expectations

Consistent with recommendations by the EEOC's *Select Task Force on the Study of Harassment in the Workplace* (U.S. Equal Employment Opportunity Commission, n.d.), it is a good idea for companies to offer workplace training which focuses on the promotion of respect, civility, safety, and fairness at work.

In addition, teaching bystanders to recognize potentially problematic behaviors can improve the sense of collective responsibility that employees feel and provide the tools and resources that bystanders need to intervene when they witness bullying or mobbing behavior. When trained properly, witnesses to problematic behaviors (e.g., supervisors, colleagues, and managers) can be an organization's most important resource in preventing and stopping this form of workplace abuse.

– Track Key Metrics and Regularly Audit Key Processes

Critical HR processes should be regularly audited and metrics should be tracked in key areas (e.g., employee complaints, employee discipline, workers' compensation claims, absenteeism, and termination). Regular monitoring of this data can serve as an "early alert" to the organization about issues that may be developing in terms of toxic bosses or workplace climates. If turnover is very high in a certain department, that can be a tell-tale sign of a problem with a manager's behavior.

Given that most lawsuits can be traced to four distinct stages of the employment relationship, there are a few specific areas of your processes that should be regularly examined. These include *hiring* (e.g., job descriptions, application forms, employment contracts, references); *employee evaluation* (e.g., performance appraisals, promotions); *employee discipline* (e.g., rule infractions, evidence, poor performance); and *termination* (e.g., comparison to other similar situations, proper warnings, complaint procedure followed, etc.)

It is important to audit these areas of your business on a regular and systematic basis to make sure that your programs, policies, practices, and procedures are working and in compliance with ever-changing laws and regulations. In addition, working with your company's legal counsel, you may also want to regularly take steps to ensure that your company follows state and federal regulations (e.g., OSHA: hazard communication program, safety manual; COBRA: notifications, termination letters; FLSA: payment of overtime; ADEA: employment applications; ERISA: written severance plan; Title VII, FMLA, ADA: job descriptions, application questions, facilities, and pre-employment tests, among others). Auditing these areas will allow you to identify weaknesses or vulnerabilities in your systems and help you to identify issues that need to be updated—either to comply with new laws and regulations, or simply to be more comprehensive.

– **Conduct Periodic Climate and/or Employee Satisfaction Surveys**
Employee satisfaction surveys are typically used by organizations to assess the "climate" of the organization—how employees are feeling about key issues related to employee engagement. This data can also serve to alert the company about problems that may be developing (e.g., leaders with high turnover in their departments, etc.). Importantly, though, action should be taken quickly to address any problems identified by the survey data. Doing so will help to generate trust among employees because they will see that the organization is taking their feedback seriously.

– **More Frequent On-Site visits by Senior Leaders**
While there are many different ways for senior leaders of an organization to get feedback about their direct reports, one of the easiest and most effective is for them to get out of their offices and visit with their direct reports (and also with their subordinates) with some degree of frequency—in their space. Taking time to go outside the comfort of the "executive zone" and physically walking around a department and talking with people is a quick way to get a sense about the morale in the department first-hand.

> I would try to tell people this—it's easy to please your boss. That's the easiest thing in the world to do because you can please your boss, piss off your peers and totally destroy your subordinates. You can do it and that boss, if he never comes and goes checks to the left and right and checks below this guy, I mean he could have the most toxic organization underneath him and that [senior] boss will never know about it.

> If you want to know the climate of your organization, talk to the people to your left and right and talk to the people below. And allow them to be honest, open and objective and then you will really get to know what your organization is like . . .

Intervention Strategies

Other strategies focused at the individual level—but which are also likely to positively affect an organization's culture—include efforts to screen, hire and promote individuals with high emotional intelligence and improvements to the competency of leaders, managers, and supervisors to lead or manage people. Some promising initiatives include:

- **Conduct Extensive Interviews and Background Investigations**

Conduct extensive interviews and background checks on potential new hires with the goal of learning as much as possible about the quality of their communication and conflict resolution skills (Aamodt, 2016, 2015). It is also a good idea to review turnover statistics in departments or divisions under the candidate's control because a high departure rate can be a potential danger signal—or at least a reason to conduct more due diligence.

- **Hire, Promote, and Train Leaders with High Emotional Intelligence**

Truly effective leaders are distinguished by a high degree of emotional intelligence (widely referred to as "EQ") which includes *self-awareness* (which includes the core competency of emotional self-awareness), *self-management* (which includes the core competencies of emotional self-control, adaptability, achievement orientation, and a positive outlook), *social awareness* (which includes the core competencies of empathy and organizational awareness), and *relationship management* (which includes the core competencies of influence, coach and mentor, conflict management, teamwork, and inspirational leadership) (Goleman, 2020, 2006, 2004; Mayer & Salovey, 1997).

An emphasis on hiring, training, and promoting leaders with high EQ can help an organization move toward the creation of a more positive workplace environment. Behavioral interviews, structured interviews, and role-playing exercises, while expensive, can also be effective screening measures to prevent a bad hire.

- **Expand Orientation Programs to Include Conduct Expectations**

The onboarding process for new hires is an ideal time to stress the organization's values and its desire to maintain an ethical and respectful culture. Asking senior leaders to make brief comments to new groups of employees about these issues can also send a strong message about cultural norms that may help to minimize the potential for future misconduct.

- **Provide Early Coaching and Management/Leadership Skills Training**

The literature supports the contention that actions taken to increase the competence of an organization's leaders to deal with toxic leaders is of critical importance (Schramm, 2016). All too often, new managers are promoted into management roles without having been provided with the requisite training to actually prepare them for the new job.

Mentoring and coaching as a part of professional development can be an important way to create strong leaders (Society for Human Resource Management, 2016). In addition, leadership training that includes a focus on emotions and interpersonal skills can help individuals improve their emotional intelligence and better understand how their behavior impacts others, which may cause them to adopt a more positive and effective management style (Kets de Vries, 2010).

– Provide Enhanced "Soft Skills" Training

Hard skills are the technical expertise and knowledge needed to perform a job, while "soft skills" are interpersonal qualities and personal attributes that an individual possesses (also referred to as "people skills"). Soft skills training focuses on the issues related to the development of greater emotional intelligence, integrity, communication, courtesy, responsibility, social skills, positive attitude, professionalism, flexibility, teamwork, and work ethic (Feffer, 2016). These skills are vital to the development of strong managers but are often missing. Executives overwhelmingly indicate that integrity and communication are the top two soft skills needed by employees in today's workplace but are often in short supply (Robles, 2012).

Toxic leaders often lack self-awareness and empathy. To remedy this deficit, emotional intelligence training should begin when an individual is named as a new supervisor and continue throughout the leader's career path.

> *I think most toxic leaders don't wake up and say, "I'm going to be toxic" . . . there's a lack of self-awareness in toxic leaders. It's important [for the organization] to say, "Here's a mirror. You're not looking so great right now."*

> *They are not self-aware so they don't really care what you think. They're not going to ask questions about how you feel. They see A to B and really don't care. Or they see A to D and don't care about B and C. They don't care the impact it has on you and they're not going to take the time out to talk to you, to get to know how you're feeling about it. The feelings are just not there.*

> *I could have been a much more effective leader had I known some of these things [about emotional intelligence and personality profile] at a younger time.*

As the next generation of talent comes through an organization's pipeline, it would be prudent to watch for attitudes or behaviors that are even "slightly toxic" to ensure that the individual is made cognizant of the problematic behaviors so that he does not continue to use such tactics.

– Modify Performance Evaluation and Reward Systems

Solicit Input from Peers and Subordinates for Annual Review (plus Next-Level Boss). The annual performance evaluation—which is a key component of how individuals are identified and selected for advancement—appears to be a promising leverage point. In most organizations, they are based on the exclusive observations and opinions of the individual's boss, but not their subordinates. Reed (2004) notes that the problem has been referred to as *"the monkeys in the trees syndrome"*:

> When the high-status monkeys look down, they see bright and smiling monkey faces beaming back at them. When the lower-status monkeys look up, they have a much different and less attractive view. [The point is that] what we see depends upon where we sit.

Current systems typically reward the achievement of results but do not solicit input about the leader's ability to motivate and manage his subordinates or maintain a positive work climate. As a result, leaders who are effective at getting results are rewarded for their short-term focus—but those who are great at developing people are often overlooked.

> *I think that there has to be some change in the way we rate people—not just looking at their results, but also looking at the means in which they achieved them.*

Consider the Results of Employee Engagement Surveys. A focus on *how* results are accomplished may also create a strong leverage point. To this end, the data collected from annual engagement and/or satisfaction surveys would provide valuable evidence as to the leader's impact on his subordinates and provide a more holistic picture of the individual and his readiness for additional responsibilities (or not).

> *I think sometimes we keep the bad leaders around and the good leaders say, "I don't want to be a part of this anymore" and they leave. And then what do you have? You've got the JV team and you've got the sub-JV team. That's not always effective for us.*

Include Dimensions of Civility, Empathy, and Kindness in Evaluations. Developing empathy in both leaders and among team members results in demonstrable improvement in many organizational outcomes such as productivity, engagement, and retention of employees at all levels. When evaluation criteria are unclear, leaders can avoid being held accountable and blame others for negative outcomes (or take credit for positive ones). It is recommended that steps be taken to incorporate measures of civility, empathy, and kindness into performance evaluation and reward systems so that employees are evaluated and rewarded not only on the results that they achieve, but also on *how* they accomplish those results (Daniel & Metcalf, 2016).

Use of 360-Degree Performance Reviews. Implementation of 360-degree performance reviews can also be an effective strategy so that leaders and managers regularly receive feedback from not only their immediate supervisor, but also from their colleagues and subordinates; however, it is generally recommended that this type of feedback be used only for purposes of employee development—not for evaluation. The importance of providing candid feedback to toxic leaders as early as possible—ideally, when the problem is first observed—cannot be overstated.

Importantly, there is widespread consensus that individuals should not be able to hand-pick the respondents. The process should be more transparent and structured in a way that the leader does not have undue influence on the feedback that he receives.

> *The only way to really solve it, of course, is a feedback system from the lower levels. Higher levels intrinsically can't see it [the toxic behavior]. The only way to really make it work is to include peer and subordinate reviews. I think you've just got to figure out where a smart cut line is . . .*

Accountability Strategies

It is also important to ensure that there is accountability for those who fail to observe behavioral norms at work. Without accountability, there can be no basis for a social order to sustain the social systems in organizations as we know them (Tetlock, 1992). Left to their own discretion, many people—aka leaders with toxic tendencies—will tend to focus on advancing their own interests rather the interests of the larger social group. When individuals perceive high levels of organizational accountability, they are likely to be more likely to control their own self-interested behavior and less likely to exploit or harm others in the organization.

To this end, some possible strategies include:

– **Establish Fair Reporting and Investigation Processes**
Internal processes designed to resolve conflict create an incentive for employees to try to resolve conflicts directly with their employer (rather than filing complaints with regulatory agencies or engaging in costly and time-consuming litigation). Implementing a system through which parties can resolve conflict inside their company creates incentives for employees to consider resolving grievances with their employer, rather than engaging in costly and time-consuming litigation. Additionally, a formal system often reduces the likelihood that employees will band together to seek union representation (if one is not already present).

From least costly and quickest to most costly and most time-consuming, following are various methods that companies are currently using with successful results:

Open-Door Policies. These are policies which encourage employees to meet with their immediate supervisor to discuss and resolve work-related issues. It is a first step. For effectiveness, the company must: (1) indicate in its policies that there will be no negative repercussions when a complaint is voiced by an employee; and (2) provide ongoing training to managers about company policies, negotiation, mediation and problem-solving.

Senior Management Review. The next step following the failure of conflict resolution with the employee's immediate supervisor via the open-door technique is to have the issue reviewed by the next higher level of the management chain. This type of review gives the employee the ability to go up the hierarchy one level (or more) to the next most senior manager.

Peer Review. The aggrieved employee is given the opportunity to present his side of a dispute to a small panel of employees and supervisors selected from a pool of employees trained in dispute resolution. The method is often successful because employees participate in the decisions that affect them, breaking down barriers between management and employees. Though policies and rules differ by organization, peer review can be made binding on both parties (or not). If it is not binding and the resolution is not satisfactory to the employee, the dispute can be submitted to mediation or arbitration.

Facilitation. An opportunity for a neutral employee within the organization to help resolve the dispute. Often the individual is an employee relations manager who acts as the key facilitator. The facilitator does not make judgments on the merits of disputes nor do they provide a final decision. Rather, he or she helps both sides decide the best way to settle the dispute.

Ombudsperson. This is an individual who generally reports to a member of the company's senior management. The "ombuds" (as these roles are typically referred to) can be a full-time employee or he can be an individual outside of the organization who the company contracts with to provide this independent investigation and mediation service. Any conversation by an ombudsperson with employees is held confidential. The ombuds can provide general information to management to help the company resolve the problem but cannot divulge specific information provided by employees.

Mediation. This method requires the use of a mediator who is a neutral third party guiding two conflicting parties in exploring innovative solutions to their dispute. Mediators can be internal employees trained in conflict management and mediation or trained or external mediators who have no perceived conflict of interest with the company. The willingness to resolve a dispute through mediation should be voluntary.

Arbitration. Arbitration is typically the most formal and costly, and frequently most time-consuming, of all ADR alternatives. It is a formal process similar in nature to a court situation where an arbitrator issues a binding decision. In arbitration, witnesses may be presented and cross-examined. One advantage to a company in arbitration is that once a decision is rendered, there is finality as there is no appeal process governed by the Federal Arbitration Act.

– **Ensure That the Risks of Bad Behavior Are Greater Than the Rewards**
Toxic leaders are likely to assess the potential risks associated with using abusive tactics against the potential benefits to be gained from their use. If the likelihood of discipline is low and the potential payoff is high (e.g., higher bonuses, promotions, etc.), bad behavior is likely to continue to be a viable strategy for personal success. As a result, it is imperative that the costs associated with mistreating others (e.g., the risk of discipline or other sanctions) outweigh the potential to personally benefit from its use through increased pay, promotions, and other rewards (Daniel & Metcalf, 2016):

> We have to have the moral courage to step up and if we see something wrong, we have to do something about it. That's our job. We have to be sure the right people are leaving our [organizations]. And [we have to] hold people accountable at all levels. When subordinates see that toxic leaders are not held accountable, they lose faith in the system and that's why they don't report things.

– Provide Early Intervention and Coaching for Abrasive Employees

If an individual should display abrasive characteristics (e.g., behaviors that do not violate company policies, but which do create tension and friction between employees), it is important to intervene early. With the help of an experienced coach, it is possible for abrasive managers to overcome their personal limitations or blind-spots—*if* they are personally willing to accept the fact that they need to change—by developing more self-awareness and learning more effective ways to interact with others; however, when coaching and confronting the individual fail to change that person's behavior, it is up to HR to counsel targets and confer with managers to decide on the appropriate disciplinary action, up to and including termination.

– Increase Accountability for Leaders to Be Involved in Employee Development

An aggressive emphasis on formal coaching, mentoring, and educating can have a positive impact on the developmental process and in future assignments and selection for promotion; however, most organizational systems provide no rewards or recognition for leaders who take the time to mentor and coach their people. As a result, whether they receive it or not is highly dependent on the interests, skills, and interest of their specific unit leader. Not surprisingly, though, mentoring and coaching, as well as related forms of development, are highly prized by subordinates at every level of an organization.

> *I think what made him a great leader in my eyes [was that] he was very passionate about what he was doing. At the time it seemed like we all thought he was kind of crazy, but now, looking back, it was I think his passion for what he was doing—developing his subordinates was one of the things that I think made him great.*

Through their actions, senior leaders must convince their subordinates that that time spent on developing others (e.g., coaching, mentoring, counseling, and training) is good for their department, as well as the organization as a whole. In so doing, they help to seed a culture where each new generation will see it as a primary responsibility to develop the next generation of employees coming up behind them.

It will be important to re-emphasize that the development of others is the hallmark of a great leader—and that rewards and promotions are based not just on getting results, but also upon their success in developing people.

– Engage in Post-Project "After Action" Reviews

The U.S. military is widely credited for creating the process of "after action reviews"—a structured review or de-brief process analyzing *what* happened, *why* it happened, and *how* it can be done better by the participants and leaders responsible for the project or event (Wikipedia, n.d.).

The implementation of a similar process within a corporate organization can create greater self-awareness among those who mistreat their employees, thus potentially creating a stronger impetus for personal behavioral change. Similarly, a review of exit interviews by employees departing the organization is another opportunity to figure out what happened and what can be done about the situation to reduce similar problems in the future.

– **Impose Real Accountability and Consequences**

Abrasive leaders should be put on notice and given a chance to correct their abusive behavior. After a reasonable period of coaching and training, though, the employment relationship should be terminated with those who are not able (or simply not willing) to change.

Organizations where mistreatment of employees is ignored or overlooked permit it (either directly or unwittingly) because it then gets normalized. In those companies, there is a substantially higher probability that the toxic leader's bad behavior will subsequently be imitated if it remains unaddressed. Why? Because it then begins to be an accepted part of the organizational culture.

The bottom line is that toxic leaders are generally responsive only to those in positions of power. As a result, if senior leaders impose accountability for engaging in bad behavior by actually relieving toxic leaders of their roles, things will most definitely change. Those with negative workplace climates will no longer be successful and it will help to ensure that their negative behaviors are not imitated by others going forward.

> We need to make an effort to show that when the [organization]has identified a toxic leader, they're going to get rid of him—not just move him to another position—but actually get rid of him. It's just like if you have a crime wave happening and people are just getting slaps on the wrist. Well, you're probably not going to stop the crime. But if some people are going to jail, then other people are going to say, well, "maybe I need to relook at myself" or, "I might be that toxic leader and the next investigation . . . might be coming down on me" . . .

Many of these practices have been described in the literature as "high-performance work practices" or "sophisticated" HR practices (Huselid, 1995). Collectively, they are generally viewed as viable strategies for creating sustainable organizational change and positive workplace climates.

Restoration and Recovery Strategies

It is most typically up to HR professionals to help targets strategize about how to handle the toxic leader's negative behavior and guide them to available resources. This can include help with coping and stress management strategies, support via employee assistance programs, access to coaching and counseling, plus information about employee benefits. The evidence clearly suggests that the provision of support to those affected by abuse at work can help to significantly reduce its negative impact on the target's ability to cope.

Some of the most promising ways to provide this support and assistance for targets include:

– **Offer Coping Skills, Conflict Resolution and Resilience Training**
The development of coping skills and resilience have been suggested as strong ways to help targets handle abusive workplace experiences. Training in interpersonal skills, conflict resolution, and stress management has been found to assist targets to cope with abusive misconduct and manage their emotions better. In addition, counselling, and rehabilitation are appropriate interventions for targets (Duffy & Sperry, 2014, 2012).

– **Establish Restorative Justice Procedures**
The implementation of restorative justice practices have also been deemed a helpful response to situations of workplace abuse. With this process, targets and abusers are brought together to discuss the harm done to the target and to identify ways to make amends and repair the relationship, including an apology from the perpetrator directly to the target. The goal of a restorative justice process is to make the target "whole" again—to the maximum extent possible (Zehr, 2001).

Conclusions

Sometimes the most difficult and protracted problems—including building a positive workplace culture and creating positive relationships with your employees—also have some of the easiest solutions. However, knowing *what* to do is much less difficult than actually *doing* it. The strategy for achieving a positive organizational culture boils down to consistently adhering to these guidelines:
– Build your organizational culture based on empathy, compassion, and caring;
– Be truthful and share frequent information with employees;
– Listen carefully to your employees when they raise issues or come to you to discuss problems—give them your full and undivided attention;
– Establish fair systems and make consistent decisions based on your policies;
– Ensure that your managers are trained to spot issues and resolve conflicts quickly; and above all,
– **Treat all employees with fairness, dignity and respect—*at all times*.**

In combination, the implementation of these strategies is an important antidote to destructive and toxic leadership practices and will help you to create a working environment where employees are motivated, engaged, and more productive—and one where the organization achieves positive outcomes as well.

References

Aamodt, M.G. (2016). *Conducting background checks for employee selection*. SHRM-SIOP Science of HR White Paper Series. https://www.shrm.org/Research/Documents/SHRM-SIOP%20Background%20Checks.pdf.

Aamodt, M.G. (2015). Using background checks in the employee selection process. In C. Hanvey & K. Sady (Eds.), *Practitioner's guide to legal issues in organizations*. Springer.

American Bar Association (2012). *Model anti-bullying policy*. http://www.americanbar.org/content/dam/aba/events/labor_law/2012/03/national_conference_on_equal_employment_opportunity_law/mw2012eeo_eisenberg2.authcheckdam.pdf.

Daniel, T.A. & Metcalf, G.S. (2016). *Stop bullying at work: Strategies and tools for HR, legal & risk management professionals* (2nd edition). SHRM Books.

Duffy, M. & Sperry, L. (2012). *Mobbing: Causes, consequences and solutions*. Oxford University Press.

Duffy, M. & Sperry, L. (2014). *Overcoming mobbing: A recovery guide for workplace aggression*. Oxford University Press.

Eisenberger, R., Huntington, R., Hutchison, S. & D. Sowa (1986). Perceived organizational support. *Journal of Applied Psychology, 71*(3), 500–507.

Einarsen, K., Mykletun, R.J., Skogstad, A., Einarsen, S. & D. Salin (2015, May 24). *Ethical infrastructure in combating unethical behavior in organizations: The case of workplace bullying*. EAWOP Conference, Oslo, Norway.

Feffer, M. (2016, April 1). HR's hard challenge: When employees lack soft skills. SHRM's *HR Magazine, 61*(3). https://www.shrm.org/publications/hrmagazine/editorialcontent/2016/0416/pages/0416-soft-skills.aspx

Gallup Organization (2015). *State of the American manager: Analytics and advice for leaders*. https://www.gallup.com/services/182138/state-american-manager.aspx.

Goleman, D. (2004, January). What makes a leader? *Harvard Business Review*. https://hbr.org/2004/01/what-makes-a-leader.

Goleman, D. (2006). *Social intelligence: The new science of human relationships*. Bantam.

Goleman, D. (2020, June 9). Harvard researcher says the most emotionally intelligent people have these 12 traits. Which do you have? *CNBC*. https://www.cnbc.com/2020/06/09/harvard-psychology-researcher-biggest-traits-of-emotional-intelligence-do-you-have-them.html.

Huselid, M. (1995). The impact of human resource management practices on turnover, productivity, and corporate financial performance. *Academy of Management Journal, 38*(3), 635–672.

Kets de Vries, M. (2010). *Developing leaders and leadership development*. INSEAD Faculty & Research Working Paper. http://sites.insead.edu/facultyresearch/research/doc.cfm?did=45346.

Lombardo, M.M. & McCall, M.W. J. (1984). *Coping with an intolerable boss*. Center for Creative Leadership.

Mayer, J.D. & Salovey, P. (1997). What is emotional intelligence? In Salovey, P. & Sluyter, D.J. (Eds.), *Emotional development and emotional intelligence: Educational implications* (pp. 3–31). Basic Books.

Nowak, K. & Zak, P. (2020). Empathy enhancing antidotes for interpersonally toxic leaders. *Consulting Psychology Journal: Practice and Research, 72*(2), 119–133.

Reed, G.E. (2004). Toxic leaders. *Military Review*, 67–71. http://www.au.af.mil/au/awc/awcgate/milreview/reed.pdf.

Robles, M.M. (2012). Executive perceptions of the top 10 soft skills needed in today's environment. *Business Communication Quarterly, 75*(4), 453–465.

Schein, E.H. (1992). *Organizational culture and leadership* (2nd ed.). Jossey-Bass.

Schramm, J. (2016, April 1). Survey: Employees lack critical competencies. SHRM's *HR Magazine*. https://www.shrm.org/publications/hrmagazine/editorialcontent/2016/0416/pages/0416-competencies-leadership.aspx.

Society for Human Resource Management (2016). *Employee satisfaction and engagement: Revitalizing a changing workforce*. https://www.shrm.org/Research/SurveyFindings/Articles/Documents/2016-Employee-Job-Satisfaction-and-Engagement-Report.pdf.

Society for Human Resource Management Foundation (2016). *Creating a more human workplace where employees and businesses thrive*. https://www.shrm.org/about/foundation/products/documents/4-16%20human%20workplace-final.pdf.

Society for Human Resource Management (2016). *SHRM survey findings: Using competencies to achieve business unit success—the executive perspective*. https://www.shrm.org/hr-today/trends-and-forecasting/research-and-surveys/Documents/SHRM%20Survey%20Findings_Using%20Competencies%20to%20Achieve%20Business%20Unit%20Success_FINAL.pdf.

Tetlock, P.E. (1992). The impact of accountability on judgment and choice: Toward a social contingency model. *Advances in Experimental Social Psychology*, *25*, 331–376.

U.S. Equal Employment Opportunity Commission (n.d.). *Select Task Force on the Study of Harassment in the Workplace*. https://www.eeoc.gov/eeoc-select-task-force-study-harassment-workplace.

Wikipedia (n.d.). *After-action reviews*. https://en.wikipedia.org/wiki/After-action_review#:~:text=An%20after%20action%20review%20(AAR,developed%20by%20the%20U.S.%20Army.

Zehr, H. (2001). *The little book of restorative justice*. http://www.unicef.org/tdad/littlebookrjpakaf.pdf.

Chapter 12
Other Institutional Guardrails: The Important Role of Organizational Policies and Reward Structures

In a world of *#MeToo* and *#Time's Up*, it is a good time to seriously review your internal policies and practices to ensure that your organization has the appropriate safeguards in place to protect employees from abuse at work while also protecting the company from potential legal liability—those all-essential *guardrails* we have considered throughout this book.

So, what should courageous HR practitioners—those of you who want to help build a more positive workplace climate—consider doing in the days and weeks ahead? It may be helpful for you to start with an audit your organization's current policies, practices, and reward structures based on a series of focused questions as outlined in this chapter (Daniel, 2020).

Then think about setting up a meeting with your senior leaders to internally discuss what you found find as a result of that review, along with your recommendations for change. You will then be well-positioned to develop an action plan (in conjunction with your legal counsel, as appropriate) to strengthen your current practices.

1 Do you have an effective anti-harassment/anti-bullying policy and complaint procedure?

At a minimum, a comprehensive policy and complaint procedure should include the following elements:
- A clear explanation of the prohibited conduct;
- An unequivocal statement that complainants will be protected from retaliation;
- A clearly described complaint process that provides accessible avenues of complaint (and preferably several different ways to make the complaint);
- Assurance that the employer will protect the confidentiality of the complainant— *to the extent possible*;
- A process that provides for a fast, thorough, and impartial investigation by an experienced investigator; and
- Assurance that the employer will take immediate and appropriate corrective action if it determines that harassment has occurred.

Importantly, it should be noted that the U.S. Equal Employment Opportunity Commission (EEOC) has recently issued guidance about promising practices to prevent harassment (U.S. Equal Employment Opportunity Commission, n.d.). These guidelines provide clear recommendations about what constitutes a comprehensive and effective harass-

https://doi.org/10.1515/9783111201771-012

ment policy and complaint system, guidance about leadership and accountability, as well as suggestions about effective training and communication practices. Employers are advised to review and consider implementing the EEOC's detailed recommendations to the maximum extent practicable.

In addition, an emerging best practice is to require "bystanders" (e.g., those who may witness the bad behavior but not be directly involved in the situation) to affirmatively notify the company of the potential problem and to intervene as may be appropriate given the facts of the situation.

2 Do you broadly and regularly disseminate the anti-harassment/anti-bullying policy and conduct expectations to employees?

Employers should provide every employee with a copy of the policy and complaint procedures and redistribute it periodically. Companies should also post it in central locations (e.g., bulletin boards, Intranet, etc.) and incorporate the policy into their code of business conduct, as well as their employee and manager handbooks. It is advisable to also require employees to sign an acknowledgment that they have read, understand, and agree to abide by the policy's terms.

In addition, communications to employees should also stress the company's expectation that employees will notify management or Human Resources immediately if they witness any behavior that even *may* be in violation of the company's policy against harassment. A common way to communicate this expectation to employees is this: *If you see something, say something; otherwise, your silence makes you complicit in perpetuating the problem.*

3 Are senior leaders actively involved in setting the tone and "culture of compliance" for the organization?

Senior leaders must be actively viewed as serious about enforcing a "culture of compliance" that includes treating all employees with dignity and respect (Daniel, 2003). If they fail to allocate appropriate time and resources for training and communication, fail to personally take the time to attend training sessions, or are seen as joking about the policy and the seriousness of the issue, it will seriously undermine the company's efforts to ensure a positive workplace environment.

It is also helpful for executives to be kick-off speakers for annual training sessions, as well as to send letters to employees, video messages, personal appearance at department meetings, company newsletters, etc. Most importantly, senior executives must model the expected behavior and quickly intervene if they see a colleague treating another employee in an inappropriate manner.

4 Do you conduct quick and thorough investigations upon receipt of a complaint of harassment or misconduct, even if it involves a senior leader?

An independent fact-finding investigation by a neutral party should be launched immediately upon receipt of a complaint. It may also be necessary to take immediate action to ensure that further abuse does not occur while the investigation is taking place (e.g., by making scheduling changes, transfer of the alleged harasser, or placing the alleged harasser on non-disciplinary leave with pay pending the conclusion of the investigation). If employees do not believe that issues of misconduct are being treated seriously by the company and its senior leaders, they are more likely to escalate their complaints by going outside of their company's reporting procedures.

5 Do you implement prompt corrective action at the conclusion of an investigation, if warranted?

Remedial measures should be designed to:
- *Stop the misconduct or abuse* (e.g., oral or written warning, transfer or reassignment, demotion, reduction of wages, suspension, discharge, training or counseling, and post-event monitoring to ensure that there is no retaliation and that the harassment has stopped);
- *Correct its effects on the employee* (e.g., restoration of leave taken by the employee because of the harassment, expungement of any negative evaluations that are unmerited, reinstatement, an apology by the harasser, monitoring treatment of the employee to ensure no retaliation occurs in the future, and other appropriate "make whole" actions appropriate to the circumstances); and
- *Ensure that the misconduct does not recur* (e.g., the discipline imposed on the harasser should be proportional to the seriousness of the offense, up to and including termination).

6 Do you provide counseling and assistance for targets of harassment, misconduct, and other forms or mistreatment and abuse?

Harassment, bullying, and similar types of abuse at work can have serious and long-lasting consequences for the individual who has been victimized. As a result, organizations should offer immediate access to qualified counselors who have been trained to diagnose and treat these types of issues in order to minimize the longer-term emotional impact that the sexual harassing incident may have on the individual.

7 Do you hold frequent and mandatory anti-harassment/ anti-bullying training sessions?

Periodic, interactive training about sexual harassment and workplace bullying, the company's policy against it, and the complaint and response process—can help to ensure that all employees and managers understand what it is and how to identify it (with examples), as well as their responsibility to act if they see it happening (e.g., notify their supervisor, HR, or senior management of the potential problem) pursuant to the company's policies and processes. Training should be provided to employees at every level and location of your organization according to federal, state, and local guidelines and regulations (which can be different in terms of required frequency and coverage of topics).

8 Do you hold expanded training sessions for supervisors and managers?

Because supervisors and managers have additional responsibilities and are generally held to a higher standard of expected conduct, there should be special training for them to make sure that they are fully aware of their duties and responsibilities to act under the company's policy and complaint procedures. Employers who demonstrate that they have fully informed all employees and managers about the policy and procedures are far more likely to resolve problems earlier as well as to avoid potential liability.

9 Do you communicate your company's expectations about expected workplace conduct at regular intervals?

In addition to re-affirming the company's harassment policy and complaint procedure, it is also recommended that regular communications to employees also reinforce the company's expectations that employees engage in civil and respectful interactions with their co-workers—at all times and regardless of role or level.

222

2

10 Do you evaluate your anti-harassment/anti-bullying policy and practices regularly?

It is advisable to undertake an annual audit of your policies and practices to ensure that they continue to comply with current laws, EEOC guidelines and recommended best practices, and to update them as necessary (U.S. Equal Employment Opportunity Commission, n.d.).

11 Do the proactive steps your organization takes to prevent harassment and bullying go beyond the minimum required by law?

Taking action that goes beyond simply what is mandated by law can help to ensure a more harassment-free workplace culture. Periodic employee surveys, training that encourages workplace civility and a respectful workplace and/or bystander intervention training, and reviews of internal metrics (e.g., complaints, increases in workers' compensation or absenteeism, etc.) are examples of proactive ways to do more than just perfunctorily issue a policy, require employees to attend an annual training session, and call it "good".

12 Do you regularly review the number of complaints and lawsuits, both cumulatively and among specific departments, in an effort to spot emerging patterns or problems?

Data related to complaints, lawsuits, workers compensation, attendance, and medical costs should be regularly reviewed to spot potential problems in certain divisions or departments or complaints against certain managers that may be developing so that preventive measures can be employed quickly.

In addition to these policy-related considerations, here are a few other ideas that you may wish to consider in order to strengthen your internal practices and further protect your company.

13 Do you conduct appropriate due diligence prior to hiring a new employee?

Due diligence should be conducted prior to most hires, not only to ensure organizational "fit" but also to determine if the candidate has a record of bad behavior. Conducting background investigations and mining the candidate's social media (e.g., photos, offensive postings, etc.) can be a rich source of information that can protect the company from making an inadvisable hiring decision.

14 Do you include provisions within your employment contracts to protect the company if an executive engages in misconduct?

If an executive is terminated for misconduct, the last thing you want is for them to walk away with a golden parachute that could be viewed as a "reward" for their bad behavior. Instead, it is advisable to include a "claw back" provision in your employment contracts that clearly states that if an individual's employment is terminated for cause (e.g., confirmed violation of company policy, sexual misconduct, financial fraud or embezzlement, etc.), then the agreement is automatically terminated, and no further payments are due.

15 Do you regularly advise senior management and your board of directors about policy changes and provide them with data about internal complaints and significant lawsuit filings?

It is suggested that both senior leaders and your board be notified about significant changes to your policy and procedures, as well as data regarding complaints and lawsuits so that they can be vigilant about identifying trends and for ensuring that preventive measures, appropriate insurance coverage, and/or regulatory disclosures are implemented.

16 Do you have procedures and an internal team in place that will help you to determine if a public disclosure is required?

Some significant terminations, resignations, or complaints (e.g., against an executive officer or board member) trigger obligations which require the company to file specific documents with the Securities and Exchange Commission (e.g., Form 8-K, proxy, etc.). Moreover, in certain cases, a public company may have an obligation to publicly disclose harassment and other misconduct claims, lawsuits or investigations, to the extent that the matter is likely to have a quantitatively or qualitatively material impact on the company,

17 Are you prepared to respond quickly if a full-blown crisis happens within your company?

It is important to be prepared to respond quickly in the event of a significant harassment complaint or termination event, especially when it involves a senior executive or member of your board of directors. Consider identifying the appropriate team of experts who should be involved and decide in advance who will have decision-making authority. Retention of a public relations and/or crisis management firm in advance is useful so that you can agree on a preliminary response protocol.

It is also highly recommended that you retain experienced outside counsel now so that they will be ready to help you sort through the complicated issues that a high-level event will trigger. In addition, auditing your practices and procedures and pro-actively reviewing employment agreements to determine relevant termination provisions on a regular basis will ensure that you are ready to appropriately respond to any significant issue that may come your way.

Depending on the sophistication of your senior leadership or the size of your company, it may turn out to be difficult to ensure that these policies and procedures are approved, implemented, and regularly audited. However, if not you, then who is best positioned within the organization to actually make it happen?

I hope you will summon the courage—and the will to sustain the effort—needed to make sure that these preventive policies and practices are in place to protect your employees, your senior leaders, and ultimately your organization.

References

Daniel, T.A. (2003, Fall). Developing a "culture of compliance" to prevent sexual harassment, *Employment Relations Today*, *30(3)*, 33–42.

Daniel, T.A. (2020). The era of #MeToo and #Time's Up: A spotlight on sexual harassment at work. In Belak, T. & Wilkin, L. (Eds.), *From discord to harmony: Making your workplace hum* (pp. 151–169). Information Age Publishing, Inc.

U.S. Equal Employment Opportunity Commission. *Promising practices for preventing harassment.* https://www.eeoc.gov/eeoc/publications/promising-practices.cfm.

U.S. Equal Employment Opportunity Commission. *Sexual harassment.* https://www.eeoc.gov/laws/types/sexual_harassment.cfm.

Strategies and Tools: Developing Better Leaders and Managers

Chapter 13
Components of Effective Leadership Development Programs

Given the prevalence of bad behavior in our organizations, we clearly need to be proactive about stopping it. The most logical thing to do is to develop individuals, through training and workshops, and teach them effective leadership behaviors, with a special emphasis on ways to motivate and inspire their people.

Recent attempts to quantify the investment indicate that leadership and management development training is a \$366 billion global industry (Training Industry, 2021). Organizations invest in leadership development because the research has consistently shown that good leadership is a critical part of organizational health, which is an important driver of shareholder returns (De Smet, Schaninger, & Smith, 2014).

So what should a leadership program focus on? Based on a survey of 81 global organizations that were diverse in geography, industry, and size, McKinsey & Company's work on their *Organizational Health Index* determined that four leadership behaviors explain 89 percent of the variance between strong and weak organizations in terms of leadership effectiveness (Westfall, 2019):
- Be supportive;
- Operate with a strong results orientation;
- Seek different perspectives; and
- Solve problems effectively.

McKinsey's research further suggests that the failure of leadership programs to achieve their desired results arises from four key problem areas:
- **Context conquers content**. Most leadership programs emphasize content, but it is actually context that matters most. Assuming that a particular curriculum or viewpoint will fit every company—regardless of size, culture, or current organizational structure—is often the first mistake.
- **Too much reflection, not enough application**. Leadership is discovered in action and demonstrated in application. What Steve Jobs did is impressive and informative, but what is right for your organization is what actually matters. Connecting concepts to current events and tying ideas to action is key.
- **Understanding culture**. No leadership training program can truly succeed unless the organization is willing to transcend the mindset that goes like this: "that's the way we've always done things".
- **What gets measured gets done**. How will you know if your leadership initiative was a success? Understanding the behaviors that are measured and how to quantify soft skills can be challenging. However, without measurement tools in place, there is simply no way to know the business impact of your leadership investment.

https://doi.org/10.1515/9783111201771-013

With this understanding of some of the key behaviors which drive leader success and some of the most common reasons for a new initiative's failure, this chapter will provide some examples of the important topical components of an effective leadership/ management and supervisory development program. Critically, though, you will need to assess any curriculum or leadership viewpoint that might be recommended for "fit". By this, I mean that you should consider its congruence with your organization's size, culture, and organizational structure, as well as your senior leadership's willingness to invest in the training and approach over the long-term.

In an effort to brainstorm and get you started, a good place to start in the development of any curriculum would be to prioritize the four areas described above which account for 89 percent of leadership effectiveness (e.g., be supportive, operate with a strong results orientation, seek different perspectives, and solve problems effectively).

In addition, here are some of the other topics you might want to consider when you undertake the development of a new program:

I Senior-Level Leadership/Management Development Program

Seasoned Judgment and Decision Making

Senior managers are responsible for making complex and far-reaching decisions. As a result, you frequently need to sort through complex issues, determine which information to use and which to discard, and also to make some tough calls. This section focuses on the development of analytical thinking skills, finding the right information, identifying the issues and making the right decisions at the right time.

Financial Acumen and Industry Knowledge

Understanding financial information and your industry are bottom-line skills for all executives. If you do not understand the numbers, you will not make the numbers. If you do not understand the basics of your industry and its trends, you will miss the boat. This section will outline some of the major areas that you need to pay close attention to and will also explain key financial concepts and ways to access industry information and intelligence.

Communicating for Results

All too often, employees are frustrated as a result of missing information or getting it too late to matter. This section focuses on communications at work and provides strate-

gies for creating an environment of "fearless" communication—where information flows freely through all layers of the organization.

Building Organizational Relationships

Managers need to know what is happening in all areas of the organization and across their industry. You cannot afford to dwell in their offices. You need to cultivate a network of relationships inside and outside the organization and relate well to colleagues at all levels. This section will address networking and offer specific tips for relating well to your boss, your peers and your direct reports.

Managing Time and Conflict

As a manager, you are pulled in multiple directions—which can lead to confusing priorities, not enough time to do everything, as well as conflict. This section will explore strategies to prioritize your competing roles, yet get the job done with a minimum of disruption and negativity.

Managing Change

Time does not stand still and things change. The most successful managers are also "real change leaders"—a new breed of radical thinkers who embrace and push organizational change and who could never be content with maintaining the status quo. This section will focus on strategies to engage the organization to get everyone to embrace new changes and perform above expectations.

Attracting and Developing Talent

In the final analysis, it all comes down to people. If your organization does not have the type of people you need or want, you will not be successful. This section will focus on selecting and developing talented employees, including specific action steps for succession management and development planning.

Empowering Others

What does empowerment really mean? This section will focus on how to develop a place where people have the latitude and authority to do their work effectively, where they feel a sense of ownership in the bottom line and where they feel recognized for their efforts.

Influencing and Negotiating

Negotiating about business priorities, resources and similar issues is a daily event. This section will focus on how to influence people to your point of view, tips on being persuasive, winning approval for your ideas, creating win-win results and negotiating the best deal possible.

Your Career and Self-Direction

What is your personal plan? Where do you want to be in the next 5 years? How are you going to get there? This section discusses ways in which you can purposefully plan your career and align it with your most deeply held values. This section also focuses on establishing work/life balance and prioritizing your time so that you can pursue what is important to you.

II Supervisory Skills Program

The Role of the Supervisor—What It Is (And Isn't)

It is often the case that when individual contributors are promoted into a supervisory role, they are uncertain as to the expectations of the new role. This section will explore the differences between being a "regular" employee and being a supervisor and discuss the changing expectations, duties and requirements of this new role.

Performance—Getting the Job Done

Being a supervisor means setting clear expectations, delegating work, communicating clearly and holding people accountable for meeting goals and objectives. This section will explore ways to ensure that your subordinates understand what to do, when to do it, and what it should look like when it is done—as well as how to give both constructive criticism and praise.

Communication at Work

True communication does not occur unless there is a mutual understanding between two people. Misunderstood messages account for countless organizational problems, errors in decision making and expensive mistakes. This section will explore various types of communication methods (with an emphasis on active listening and non-verbal communication), and how to ensure that open and candid communication is occurring within your workplace.

Delegation, Power and Empowerment

The most frequent mistake that new supervisors make is failing to delegate and empower their subordinates. They tend to want to "do it myself" to ensure positive results; however, this can lead to a frustrated and cynical workforce. This section will focus on skill-building to help you understand that it is not only proper, but that to be a good supervisor, it is your responsibility to delegate work to your subordinates and to empower them to make decisions within certain established parameters.

Time Management

New supervisors often have a difficult time managing a myriad of new duties and following up on project progress, leaving no work time for reflection and analysis—and often have no personal time to "re-charge their batteries". This section will explore strategies to make more efficient use of your time at work, leaving you more time to focus on the truly important things in both work and life, not just the "urgent" ones that often turn into time wasters.

Conflict Resolution

If you are a human, there is no way to escape having conflict with others from time to time—both at home and at work. This section will explore ways to engage in healthy conflict and debate that can result in a "win-win" for both parties to the situation.

High-Performance Motivation

One of the primary duties of a supervisor is to establish a climate that motivates and inspires employees. This section will explore various methods that can help to create an environment where employees are motivated and want to come to work, many of which are very low cost.

Making Your Meetings More Productive

One of the key time wasters at work is meetings that are not organized or run efficiently. This section will work on skills to help you run a productive and organized meeting—one that starts with a focused and manageable agenda, starts and ends on time, recognizes each individual's contribution, yet keeps the issues moving and gets results.

Persuasive Presentation Skills

Every time you have an idea and need to persuade your manager to adopt it, you are making a presentation. Presentations occur every day, sometimes formally to your senior management team and sometimes more informally—to your manager or colleague in the hallway or elevator, or maybe over lunch. This section will focus on skills to help you present your ideas more persuasively and skillfully within your organization to get the results you want.

Avoiding Legal Landmines

There are countless regulations that govern the employment relationship. As a supervisor, you need to be able to "spot" issues before they turn into legal problems for your company. This section will provide you with an overview of your duties and responsibilities under current laws and regulations so that you can avoid legal problems for yourself and your company.

References

De Smet, A., Schaninger, B. & M. Smith (2014, April). The hidden value of organizational health—and how to capture it. *McKinsey Quarterly*. https://www.mckinsey.com/~/media/McKinsey/Business%20Func tions/Organization/Our%20Insights/The%20hidden%20value%20of%20organizational%20health% 20and%20how%20to%20capture%20it/The%20hidden%20value%20of%20organizational%20health. pdf.

Training Industry (2021). *Size of the training industry*. https://trainingindustry.com/wiki/learning-services- and-outsourcing/size-of-training-industry/.

Westfall, C. (2019). Leadership development is a $366 billion industry: Here's why most programs don't work. *Forbes*. https://www.forbes.com/sites/chriswestfall/2019/06/20/leadership-development-why-most-programs-dont-work/?sh=1264f0fd61de

Suggested Resources

Center for Creative Leadership https://www.ccl.org/
International Leadership Association http://www.ila-net.org/Resources/LPD/index.htm

Chapter 14
Practical Tools for Developing Better Leaders and Managers

In addition to the creation of more formalized leadership and management development programs, there are also other ways to improve leadership effectiveness. The exercises outlined in this chapter are designed to encourage individuals to engage in self-assessment during an internal workshop, department meeting, or leadership development program. You might consider using these tools to help your leaders and managers develop critical self-awareness and to make concrete plans for future improvement.

I Individual Exercise- Evaluating Your Personal Leadership Results

Consider a few of your *low* points related to being a leader. Reflect on these times. What can you learn about yourself from these low points? Write down at least two lessons.

_____

_____

_____

_____

_____

Consider some of your *high* points related to being a leader. Reflect on these times. What can you learn about yourself from these high points? Write down at least two lessons.

_____

_____

_____

_____

_____

On the continuum below, place an "x" on the line that indicates your level of personal satisfaction with the leader you have become.

←---→

Very Dissatisfied   Very Satisfied

https://doi.org/10.1515/9783111201771-014

What would improve your satisfaction level with yourself?

_____
_____
_____

What lessons from both your low and high points should you try to incorporate into your future leadership?

Low:_____
_____

High:_____
_____

II Individual Exercise- Your Most "Inspired Self"

Write a letter to your most inspired self. What qualities do you see that you most admire about yourself? Why do people like to work with and/or for you? Why have you been selected to be the leader or manager?

_____
_____
_____
_____
_____
_____
_____
_____
_____
_____
_____
_____
_____
_____
_____
_____
_____
_____

How often do you think you _are_ this most inspired self/leader?

__ All of the time __ Most of the time __ Some of the time __ Rarely

What obstacles keep you from being this leader all of the time?

_____

_____

_____

_____

_____

Suggested Additional Resources

Reflected Best Self Exercise https://positiveorgs.bus.umich.edu/cpo-tools/rbse/
Best Possible Self Exercise https://ggia.berkeley.edu/practice/best_possible_self

Building the Future of Work

Chapter 15
An Idealized Vision for a Great Place to Work

We have covered a lot of territory so far and much of it has focused on what is *wrong* with our workplaces. In this chapter, we will turn our attention to some of the things we can do to improve employee mental health and well-being by strengthening our organizational cultures and relationships at work and at home.

As noted previously, in 2022, the U.S. Surgeon General issued *The Framework for Workplace Mental Health & Well-Being* (U.S. Surgeon General, 2022). This landmark report acknowledged the significant impact that unhealthy workplaces were having on employee well-being and outlined a framework to positively impact the situation. Think of it as a roadmap for building a healthy and non-toxic culture. The framework identified five essential ingredients for creating and sustaining a healthy workplace:

1. **Protection from harm**: Prioritizing workplace safety, allowing for adequate rest, and normalizing and supporting mental health.
2. **Connection and community**: Creating a culture of inclusion and belonging, fostering collaboration and teamwork, and cultivating trusted relationships.
3. **Work-life harmony**: Making schedules more flexible and predictable, increasing paid leave access, respecting boundaries between work and non-work, and proving more autonomy on how work should be done.
4. **Mattering at work**: Engaging workers in workplace decisions, building a culture of gratitude and recognition, connecting individual work with the organizational mission, and providing a living wage rather than a minimum wage.
5. **Opportunity for growth**: Providing relevant and reciprocal feedback, offering quality training and education, and providing clear paths for career advancement.

Guides about how to better understand each of these components and their benefits, as well as how to successfully implement them, are further explained in the report. This framework is based on evidence-based practices which are intended to inform organizations across workplace of varied size and industries to apply to their organizations. It can be used to help leaders, managers, and supervisors, as well as empower employees, to identify and communicate with each other about organizational changes that are needed and how best to prioritize those actions.

In combination with the suggested guardrails and other ideas you have been reading about in this book, I hope you will consider each of these components and how you might put them into action within your organization. Creating a plan to enact these practices can help strengthen the essentials of workplace well-being. Every company will have unique and creative ways of implementing them, but the goal is to intentionally put into practice at least some combination of these essentials

https://doi.org/10.1515/9783111201771-015

so that employees and your organization have the potential to thrive at the highest levels.

With these five essentials in mind, now is probably a good time to put it all together to re-imagine what work could be like if it were designed in a way that inspires and really works for the people working in it.

HR leaders are responsible for ensuring that culture management is a core focus of their organization's strategy. In carrying out this essential role, HR can significantly influence the organizational norms, values, policies and procedures, communications, pay structure, employee development opportunities, pathways to resolve conflict, as well as the organization's reward and recognition systems—all of which combine to support the workplace climate your organization aspires to create and sustain.

What would an ideal organization look like from your perspective? I know that it is not realistically possible to actually start from scratch. So, the question then becomes: *what are you going to do—right now—to accelerate your organization's efforts to create a more positive workplace culture?* Developing an action plan based on your vision for the future is key.

Designing a Powerfully Positive Workplace Culture

Based on the voluminous scholar-practitioner research that has been reported on throughout this book, as well as my own research and personal work experiences, here are some concrete ideas about what an ideal workplace might include:
- A positive work environment—one that is ethical, respectful, flexible, fair, and inclusive;
- Capable leaders who inspire trust and who are uncompromisingly ethical and fair;
- Supportive and competent management who continuously coach and develop employees;
- Opportunities to do work that feels meaningful and the ability to "own" the job;
- Frequent, transparent, and honest communication;
- Recognition and appreciation for good work;
- Opportunities for employees to grow and develop; and
- Accountability.

We will further examine and expand upon each of these components next.

A positive work environment—one that is ethical, respectful, flexible, fair, and inclusive

A positive organizational climate is one that is ethical, values its employees, treats them humanely, and where respect for every employee is demonstrated *for* and demanded *from* all who work there—at all times. In addition, positive cultures offer flexibility, recognition and appreciation, and they are also fair and inclusive. These measures are no longer HR strategies; they are absolute business imperatives.

Capable leaders who inspire trust and who are uncompromisingly ethical and fair

Through their consistent words and actions, leaders who are ethical and fair inspire us and create a sense of trust throughout the organization. They also ensure that employees understand the company's vision, mission, and purpose—and their place in it —which creates a more engaged and committed workforce. The best leaders help others to achieve things they didn't think were possible. As a result, they are also constantly engaged in the development of their people and consistently operate with the long-term best interests of the organization top of mind.

Supportive and competent management who continuously coach and develop employees

The research we have examined throughout this book clearly demonstrates that an individual's immediate supervisor is the single largest determinant of engagement and job satisfaction. As a result, it is mission critical to have managers and supervisors who are well prepared for the role before they are "thrown to the wolves" to "sink or swim" as is the case in far many organizations. Once in the role, their primary function must be to coach and develop their subordinates to ensure their effectiveness in both their current role and to get them ready for their next one.

Opportunities to do work that feels meaningful and which allows people to "own" the job

At its essence, people go to work to earn a paycheck to take care of the basic necessities of life. But many of us work so that we can contribute to something bigger than ourselves and be part of a larger collective. For work to be meaningful, it must play to the strengths of the person inhabiting the role, provide opportunities to build strong connections and relationships, and also allow for the individual to "own" the job by bringing their own unique personality to the workplace. Being recognized, valued, and appreciated for their special contributions enhances trust and also increases both employee commitment and engagement.

Frequent, transparent, and honest communication

Think of communication as the "glue" that holds all of this together. When leaders, managers, and supervisors communicate frequently through transparent and honest messages, they enhance employee trust. This increased trust translates to employees who work harder and are more loyal to the organization.

Recognition and appreciation for good work

Recognition and appreciation for employee efforts are ways to keep a culture healthy and functioning. For this to happen, meaningful interactions and praise must be regular parts of the everyday work environment and not saved up for some special once-a-year ceremony. When employees feel valued and appreciated—and issues are handled fairly—they feel "psychologically safe" at work, they are more committed, and they are also able to focus and perform at a higher level.

Opportunities for employees to grow and develop

Companies thrive by attracting and retaining talented employees. Opportunities for continuous growth and development not only help employees to keep learning and up-skilling, but they also ensure that the organization will continue to ensure that its pipeline of great people is constantly replenished.

Accountability

Lastly, but of critical importance, is the imposition of accountability—consequences not only for achieving results, but also for *how* those results happen. It is a key factor in ensuring that employees observe organizational norms and that violators are not tolerated (at least for long). Swift consequences for those who do not follow established policies, rules, and organizational norms help to create a more just workplace. When that is the case, employees have more confidence that everyone will be treated fairly. It also signals to the organization that the policies and norms are so important that no one is exempted from accountability for adhering to them. Absolutely no one.

Conclusions

So, there you have it—an idealized view of a powerfully positive workplace culture. With these pillars in place, there is no denying that this kind of an environment would be my idea of the "perfect" place to work.

Although we all have enough real-world experience to realistically conclude that there will never really be a perfect workplace, I feel blessed to have had the opportunity to work for some pretty good ones (and I hope that you have too). While all of these components may not actually be achievable, at least perhaps not at the same time, they can serve as aspirational goals to inspire us to move in a more positive direction, both individually and organizationally.

Reference

U.S. Surgeon General's Framework for Workplace Mental Health & Well-Being (2022, October 22). U.S. Department of Health and Human Services. https://www.hhs.gov/surgeongeneral/priorities/ workplace-well-being/index.html.

Chapter 16
Work Shouldn't Hurt: Hopeful Signs for the Future

In the preceding chapters, you have been presented with overwhelming evidence about toxic leaders. Here is what we know: they permeate the highest levels of most organizations in fairly large numbers, they are destructive, and they cause significant and lasting damage to both people and organizations. Despite these hard facts, there is still reason to be optimistic about the future.

There have been a number of recent examples of progress, both in our workplaces and in society at-large. The U.S. Army has relieved numerous high-ranking toxic officers for creating negative toxic command climates in recent years. Numerous top corporate executives at Nike have been forced to resign due to workplace misconduct (Zwerdling, 2014). Moreover, the *#MeToo* movement (focused on ending sexual misconduct at work) has also gained momentum and received significant funding from the *#TIME'S UP* Legal Defense Fund (n.d.) to assist affected women in their legal efforts to bring their complaints forward (#MeToo Movement, n.d.).

Conversations are occurring with increased regularity on social media and in corporate boardrooms about what constitutes appropriate workplace conduct. The days of complicit silence and of ignoring the "elephant in the room" appear to be ending. Numerous organizations have terminated high-flying senior executives for their abusive behavior at work, despite their senior status or the fact that they were getting results.

Although the standards for accountability may be in flux, this much is now crystal clear: eradicating toxic leaders from our workplaces has risen in terms of priority and can no longer be the sole responsibility of HR practitioners. It is everyone's job— and it will take all of us working together to have even a remote chance of creating the types of organizations that will allow each of us to thrive and flourish. It clearly won't be easy, but it is a future that is worthy of the collective use of our time to try to make happen.

Great employees deserve great leaders and managers who cultivate a positive workplace culture. Really smart organizations have already figured out that they will not be able to attract and retain really great people by allowing any of them to be treated badly. That heavy-handed "do as I say because I said so" style of leadership is uninspiring, demoralizing, and often destructive—which is why, thankfully, it is rapidly going the way of the dinosaur. HR practitioners are front and center in making that new day—when work doesn't hurt because of abusive leaders—actually happen.

So, here's a word to the wise: a new day is coming when toxic leaders will be viewed as irrelevant relics of a long ago past—the workplace equivalent of dinosaur fossils. In many advanced organizations, that day is already here. The choice for toxic leaders and other types of destructive high performers is now clear: *change or become extinct.*

https://doi.org/10.1515/9783111201771-016

Enlightened companies understand that employees work at their best when they are treated with trust, respect, and fairness—timeless values that really matter to people and which will never go out of style. At the same time, organizations are waking up to the fact that abusive leaders drive away talent, making them bad for business and simply too expensive to keep—regardless of their ability to deliver results. The new strategy emerging as a best practice when it comes to dealing with destructive leaders goes something like this: *"Find them, fix them, or fire them"* (Owens, 2014).

This book began with an appeal from SHRM's CEO to practitioners about the importance of making culture a top HR priority (Society for Human Resource Management, 2019). I think it bears repeating here:

> Billions of wasted dollars. Millions of miserable people. It's not a warzone—it's the state of the American workplace. Toxicity itself isn't new. But now that we know the high costs and how managers can make workplaces better, there's no excuse for inaction.

I couldn't agree with him more. The research unequivocally confirms that creating and sustaining a positive workplace climate is not just the right thing to do, it is also a business imperative. When an organization has a strong and inclusive culture, three things happen for employees: they can reliably anticipate how they should act in various situations, they know that they can trust their leaders and feel confident that their problems will be handled fairly and ethically, and they know they will be rewarded and appreciated for demonstrating the organization's values.

Armed now with an abundance of new knowledge and, hopefully, some inspiration and concrete ideas for how to implement real and positive change to improve your culture and reduce the likelihood that toxic leaders can exist for very long there, what are you waiting for? Your organization needs you to step up and lead now more than ever!

References

#MeToo Movement (n.d.). https://metoomvmt.org/.

Owens, D.M. (2014, March 1). Dr. David Posen's prescription for work stress. SHRM's *HR& Magazine, 59*(3), 44.

Society for Human Resource Management (2019, September 25). *Press release.* https://www.shrm.org/about-shrm/press-room/press-releases/pages/shrm-reports-toxic-workplace-cultures-cost-billions.aspx.

#TIME's UP Legal Defense Fund (n.d.). https://timesupfoundation.org/work/times-up-legal-defense-fund/.

Zwerdling, D. (2014, January 6). Army takes on its own toxic leaders. *NPR News.* http://www.npr.org/2014/01/06/259422776/Army-takes-on-its-own-toxic-leaders.

Appendices

Appendix I
Design of the Foundational Research Study for this Book

Overview of the Study and Method

This study was designed to help the U.S. Army make better distinctions between toxic leaders who are abusive, high-performing leaders who are simply tough bosses, and those individuals who are truly exceptional leaders. The design for this study involves a qualitative strategy of inquiry using constructivist, grounded theory as the method (Charmaz, 2006). The constructivist ontological foundation for theory building places priority on the phenomena of study and sees both data and analysis as created from shared experiences and relationships with participants and other sources of data (Lee, Mitchell, & Sablynski, 1999).

Rationale for Method Selection

Lee, Mitchell, and Sabylnski (1999) describe four purposes for qualitative research that have implications for the study of leadership: theory generation, theory elaboration, theory testing, and critical theory development. Moreover, the use of a qualitative approach and, specifically, the selection of grounded theory as a methodology, is strongly advocated for leadership research (Bryman, 2004; Conger & Toegel, 2002; Conger, 1998; Parry, 1998; Van Maanen, 1983).

In particular, the method allows for theory that is inductively derived and emerges from, and is *grounded in*, the experiences of those living the phenomenon of interest (Glaser, 1978; Strauss & Corbin, 1990). What this means is that the theory is discovered, developed, and provisionally verified through systematic data collection and analysis of data pertaining to that phenomenon. Therefore, data collection, analysis, and theory development stand in reciprocal relationship with each other.

Conger and Toegel (2002) provide further support for the selection of this approach. They stress that qualitative methods are an important tool for the study of leadership for three key reasons: (1) this tool can help us understand how leadership is differentially exercised at various organizational levels; (2) given that leadership is a dynamic process, qualitative research methods can add depth and richness that is lacking in data gleaned from questionnaires; and (3) because leadership is considered by some researchers and theories to be a socially constructed role, qualitative methods can aid in understanding the construct from multiple perspectives.

Moreover, grounded theory " . . . helps researchers understand complex social processes," and is particularly appropriate when exploring relatively new concepts in

https://doi.org/10.1515/9783111201771-017

more depth (Suddaby, 2006). In fact, key paradigm shifts in the study of leadership have come from qualitative studies (Conger & Toegel, 2002; Bennis & Nanus, 1985; Mintzberg, 1973).

Grounded theory provides a detailed, rigorous, and systematic method of analysis, which has the advantage of reserving the need for the researcher to conceive preliminary hypotheses. As a result, it provides greater freedom to explore the research area and allow issues to emerge (Bryant, 2002), making it particularly useful in providing rigorous insight into areas that are relatively unknown by the researcher.

Charmaz (2006, p. 128) explains the importance of theorizing in a grounded theory study as follows:

> Theories flash illuminating insights and make sense of murky musings and knotty problems. The ideas fit. Phenomena and relationships between them you only sensed beforehand become visible. Still, theories can do more. *A theory can alter your viewpoint and change your consciousness. Through it, you can see the world from a different vantage point and create new meanings of it.* Theories have an internal logic and more or less coalesce into coherent forms.

She also suggests that theorizing "entails the practical activity of engaging the world and of constructing abstract understanding about and within it" (p. 128). As a result, the fundamental contribution of grounded theory methods resides in the fact that it can infuse a study with the tools to "bring meanings into view" (p. 129), which was a key intent of this study.

Finally, as noted by Lee (1999), while qualitative research "is not well suited for issues of prevalence, generalizability, and calibration," it *is* highly useful for purposes such as theory generation or elaboration. For those reasons, it was decided that this approach was the most appropriate one for this exploratory study.

Data Collection

Sample Selection

The selection process relied on non-probability, purposive sampling and targeted a specific population believed to possess knowledge about the topic of toxic leadership (Creswell, 2013). To be included in the study, the participants were required to meet these criteria:
(1) Hold a rank of Sergeant First Class and above, and
(2) Be either currently active or retired within the past five years.

The rationale for restricting participation to officers who met these criteria was founded on our belief that individuals at more senior ranks would have had more years of service, and therefore more opportunities to have worked for multiple leaders. We believed that this experience would provide for a more robust and well-rounded perspective of the problem. We also included only active or recently retired officers so that the perspectives offered would be limited to the U.S. Army as it exists in its current state.

Semi-Structured Interviews

A series of in-depth interviews were conducted with forty-four (44) officers in the U.S. Army. Thirty-two (32) of the interviews took place in person with active duty Army Majors and captains attending the Command and General Staff College located in Fort Leavenworth, Kansas. Three (3) additional interviews with this group were scheduled following the site visit and took place by telephone. Nine (9) additional at-large interviews of officers meeting the required sample criteria were conducted by telephone.

Fourteen (14) questions were used as prompts in an effort to help participants more directly respond to the primary research questions. Follow up questions were asked as necessary to confirm accuracy of understanding and to elaborate on statements of particular interest. Participants were provided an opportunity at the end of the interview to ask questions or offer additional comments on related issues that they considered to be important. Interviews continued until the researchers had identified clear signals of data saturation which included repetition of information and the confirmation of emerging conceptual categories (Suddaby, 2006).

Each interview lasted approximately one hour, was tape-recorded after receiving informed consent and demographic information from each participant, and was transcribed verbatim by a professional transcriptionist who had previously signed a confidentiality agreement. The interviews resulted in written transcripts totaling 464 single-spaced pages, 266,537 words, and 20,405 lines of data for coding and analysis.

Analysis of the Data

The analysis, interpretations, and conclusions about the data were conducted in accordance with the constructivist, grounded theory methodology outlined by Charmaz (2006), using constant comparative analysis. The resulting theory is an interpretation given that it is, in part, dependent on the researcher's view of the data. Using this approach gave priority to showing "patterns and connections rather than to linear reasoning" and did not attempt to determine causality (p. 126).

The main components of the grounded theory method include:
- Simultaneous involvement in data collection and analysis;
- Constructing analytic codes and categories from data, not from preconceived logically deduced hypotheses;

- Using the constant comparison method, which involves making comparisons during each stage of the analysis;
- Advancing theory development during each step of data collection and analysis;
- Memo writing to elaborate categories, specify their properties, define relationships between categories and identify gaps;
- Sampling aimed toward theory construction, not for population representativeness; and
- Conducting the literature review after developing an independent analysis.

The doctoral research assistants read the early transcripts from the initial data collection phase and provided input from their initial coding of the data against which the later coding was compared. The principal investigators read through the transcripts numerous times to ensure accuracy and then independently and separately coded the data by hand (Lincoln & Guba, 1985). The codes that emerged were reviewed by both authors and the coding process was guided by the research questions. Any disagreements were resolved through ongoing discussions until consensus was reached about all codes and categories.

During the process, our central goal was to look for similar patterns of description. As a result, we systematically compared each new description of great leaders, toxic leaders and tough bosses with former ones to decide whether it fit into an existing category or represented a new one. We met frequently to discuss our independent coding of the interview transcripts and the emerging categories. We also wrote theoretical and interpretative memos about the main themes that were emerging from our review of the data.

During the first cycle of *open coding*, we held closely to the data and consciously avoided using categories that were too abstract. This provided us freedom and openness to creatively look for new ideas and patterns emerging from the data instead of relying on earlier concepts suggested by other researchers (Charmaz, 2006). This phase of the analysis allowed us to generate preliminary categories.

For the second cycle of *axial coding*, codes that described similar behaviors were grouped into more general and abstract units of analysis. This had the effect of reducing the large number of initial codes (286 discrete codes for tough bosses and 575 discrete codes for toxic leaders) into a much smaller number of categories—specifically, this cycle resulted in the development of a total of 18 categories for toxic leaders and 14 categories for tough bosses. This phase of the analysis allowed us to further abstract the categories and begin to link them.

Analytic memo writing was used to record our observations as we analyzed the data and to diagram potential relationships between concepts. Memos helped us to capture thoughts, make comparisons and connections, and also helped to crystallize questions and potential new directions to pursue (Charmaz, 2006). This method of recording research notes—both conceptually and descriptively—allowed us to link raw data with theoretical thinking and also assisted in the overall data analysis and reporting. Memo writing forced connections among concepts and resulted in the discovery of patterns, thereby helping to generate a more complex theory, rather than just a simple description of the data.

A second review of the existing literature was conducted as a part of the memo sorting process. This helped to ensure which literature was relevant and if any additional literature should be included in the study. We answered that question in the affirmative, incorporating some new studies into the overview of current knowledge on the topic.

In the final phase of *theoretical coding and analysis*, the data was synthesized and the theoretical and interpretative memos and categories were integrated. It was at this time that we attempted to refine the categories into their highest levels of analytical meaning (Strauss & Corbin, 1990). This resulted in 5 primary categories for each type of leader. Through this iterative process, there was a cyclic interplay between data collection, analysis, and theory building (Parry, 1998). Further abstraction and interpretive rendering resulted in the emergence of the theory and conceptual model which are discussed at length elsewhere in this book.

Evaluation of the Study's Results

Qualitative research does not yield quantitative data so it does not follow the same rules for testing reliability and validity. This does not mean, though, that qualitative research need not be rigorous in its approach to the evaluation of a study's results. Strauss and Corbin (1998) provide eight criteria to assess the empirical grounding of a study:

1. Are concepts generated?
2. Are the concepts systematically related?
3. Are there many conceptual linkages, and are the categories well developed? Do the categories have conceptual density?
4. Is variation built into the system?
5. Are the conditions under which variations can be found built into the study and explained?
6. Has the process been taken into account?
7. Do the theoretical statements seem significant, and to what extent?
8. Does the theory stand the test of time and become part of the discussions and ideas exchanged among relevant social and professional groups?

At the conclusion of the study, the research findings were evaluated to ensure the empirical grounding of the study according to these criteria. With the exception of whether or not the theory will stand the test of time and become part of future academic conversations (which only time will tell), we have concluded that these criteria were met. In addition, a completed grounded theory must meet the following criteria:

a close fit with the data, usefulness, and conceptual density, durability over time, modifiability, and explanatory power (Glaser & Strauss, 1967). The study's findings were also reviewed to ensure that they were consistent with this reasoning.

This study resulted in the development of a theory which allows us "to cut through ordinary explanations and understandings and to attend to certain realities and not to others", so we also tested the validity of the theory (Charmaz, 2006). To do this, it was necessary to determine "how well that abstraction fits with the raw data" (Strauss & Corbin, 1998). This was done by comparing the conceptual model back to the raw open coding data. Upon completion of this review, it appeared that the model incorporated and fit well with the raw data.

Caution about Using these Results

It should be noted that rather than contributing verified knowledge, grounded theories seek to offer *"plausible explanations"* of the data that they have collected (Charmaz, 2006). As a result, other researchers clearly may have developed a different understanding of the data given that "the properties of the categories remain implicit until theoretical sampling and interpretive rendering [of the researcher] make them explicit" (Charmaz, 2006). Having said that, we believe that the theory and conceptual model created in this study has made a substantial contribution to both knowledge and practice that will, hopefully, prove to be useful to the U.S. Army and others.

References

Bennis, W. & Nanus, B. (1985). *Leaders: The strategies for taking charge*. Harper & Row.

Bryant, A. (2002). Re-grounding grounded theory. *Journal of Information Technology: Theory and Application*, *4*(1), 25–42.

Bryman, A. (2004). Qualitative research on leadership: A critical but appreciative review. *The Leadership Quarterly*, *15*, 729–769.

Charmaz, K. (2006). *Constructing grounded theory: A practical guide through qualitative analysis*. Sage.

Creswell, J. (2013). *Qualitative inquiry and research design: Choosing among five traditions*. Sage.

Conger, J.A. (1998). Qualitative research as the cornerstone methodology for understanding leadership. *Leadership Quarterly*, *9*, 107–121.

Conger, J., & Toegel, G. (2002). Action learning and multi-rater feedback as leadership development interventions: Popular but poorly deployed. *Journal of Change Management*, *3*(4), 332–348.

Glaser, B.G. (1978). *Theoretical sensitivity: Advances in the methodology of grounded theory*. Sociology Press.

Glaser, B.G., & Strauss, A.L. (1967). *The discovery of grounded theory*. Aldine.

Lee, T. W., Mitchell, T. R., & Sablynski, C. J. (1999). Qualitative research in organizational and vocational psychology: 1979-1999. *Journal of Vocational Behavior*, *55*, 161–187.

Lincoln, Y.S., & Guba, E.G. (1985). *Naturalistic inquiry*. Sage.

Mintzberg, H. (1973). *The nature of managerial work*. Harper & Row.

Parry, K.W. (1998). Grounded theory and social process: A new direction for leadership research. *Leadership Quarterly, 9*(1), 85–105.

Van Maanen, J. (1983). Epilogue: Qualitative methods reclaimed. In J. Van Maanen (Ed.), *Qualitative methodology* (pp. 247–268). Sage.

Strauss, A.I. & Corbin, J. (1990). *Basics of qualitative research: Grounded theory procedures and tasks.* Sage.

Strauss, A.I.& Corbin, J. (1998). *Basics of qualitative research: Techniques and procedures for developing grounded theory* (2nd Ed.). Sage.

Suddaby, R. (2006). What grounded theory is not. *Academy of Management Journal, 49*, 633–642.

Appendix II
Executive Summary: A Focus on *Toxic Leaders* and *Tough Bosses*

Purpose—This study was designed to help the Army make better distinctions between toxic leaders who are abusive, high-performing leaders who are simply tough bosses, and those who are truly exceptional leaders. The overarching aim was to more readily identify the characteristics of toxic leaders so that they can be coached to change or relieved of command before the damage to their unit is too great. In addition, the study examined the military environment to determine if there are characteristics which tend to inadvertently encourage or promote toxic leaders and/or abusive behaviors. The study also explored the actions—both individual and systemic—that can be taken to minimize or eliminate toxic leadership.

Design/Methodology/Approach—This empirical, qualitative study consisted of a series of in-depth, semi-structured interviews with 44 officers of the U.S. Army conducted during the summer and fall of 2014. Thirty-five of the interviews took place in person or by telephone with officers attending the Command and General Staff College in Fort Leavenworth, Kansas, while nine of the interviews were conducted with other military personnel meeting the sample criteria. The analysis, interpretations, and conclusions about the data were conducted in accord with the constructivist, grounded theory methodology, using constant comparative analysis.

Findings—Forty of the participants (91%) report that they had either personally worked with or observed a toxic leader at some point in their career; conversely, 100% of the participants were also able to identify one or more leaders who were exceptional. Thirty-two of the officers (72.7%) had witnessed an individual being promoted to a position of increased responsibility despite being widely perceived by subordinates to be a toxic leader. A total of 31 officers (70.4%) had given an early departure from the Army serious consideration as a result of their personal experience with a toxic leader. While 68.2% of the participants indicated that the use of toxic behaviors is never useful or positive, nearly a third (31.8%) suggested that these types of behaviors might be advantageous in certain limited situations.

The study's participants described toxic leaders as:

- *Excessively concerned about self* (e.g., promoting themselves at the expense of the organization, working the system to maximize personal advantage, taking credit for the work of others);
- *Lacking care and concern for their subordinates* (e.g., not interested in getting to know soldiers as people, abusive and malicious personal attacks, failure to engage in mentoring, coaching, or development, infrequent communication, transactional view of soldiers, creation of in and out groups);

https://doi.org/10.1515/9783111201771-018

– *Having low emotional intelligence* (e.g., frequent emotional outbursts, lack of self-awareness, failure to listen, low empathy, and developing a climate of fear); and
– *Achieving results with a short-term emphasis* (but with no regard for how those results are obtained or the impact on people), leading to a negative command climate.

Conversely, they described tough bosses as:
– *Concerned about their soldiers* (e.g., treating them with respect, compassionate, supportive and approachable);
– *Focused on the development of their subordinates* (e.g., mentor, coach, counsel, offer honest and constructive feedback, and allowing freedom to maneuver);
– *Having high emotional intelligence* (e.g., empathetic, calm under pressure, actively listens to and seeks input from others, highly self-aware, establishes climate of mutual trust and respect); and
– *Achieving results with a long-term emphasis* (e.g., high standards for self and others, tough but fair in approach, holds people accountable, high regard for organizational impact, and leads from the front), leading to a positive command climate.

This study supported the theory that toxic leaders have a *personalized* power orientation given their general need for control, their excessive self-interest, and their willingness to work long hours to gain support and to achieve their goals—but at the expense of the organization and their subordinates. Conversely, tough bosses have a *socialized* power orientation given their willingness to transcend their own self-interest and sacrifice in order to achieve the mission *and* collective good of their people and the Army as a whole.

The study identified several *potential contributing factors* that may inadvertently lead to or promote the use of toxic behaviors:
– A relentless focus on mission accomplishment;
– Senior leaders who are unaware of, or ambivalent toward, the problem;
– Lack of emphasis on the development of subordinates due to competing priorities for time (resulting in infrequent mentoring and an absence of regular performance feedback);
– Failure to address the root cause resulting in "toxic migration" of toxic leaders to other parts of the organization;
– An organizational culture which values loyalty and discourages the reporting of toxic leaders;
– Imitation of successful leaders who are toxic; and
– A cut-throat and highly competitive culture that lacks strong checks and balances.

The study's participants also identified changes to current systems, policies, and processes that are most likely to minimize or eliminate toxic leadership in the military. These included:

- Increased leader emphasis on and accountability for officer development (e.g., more mentoring and coaching, more one-on-one conversations, regular feedback on performance, and the development of reward and recognition mechanisms for officers who excel in subordinate development and consequences for those who do not);
- Changes to the officer evaluation report (e.g., to include input from not only the individual's senior officer, but also a random sampling of his peers and subordinates, plus review and consideration of recent command climate survey data);
- Changes to the promotion process (e.g., consider input from multiple levels, examine the results of command climate surveys, and solicit input from prior senior officers);
- Increased emphasis on and accountability for conducting sensing sessions and the regular use of command climate surveys (e.g., require surveys to be conducted on a regular basis, act on the data to ensure accountability and improve trust, and increase the frequency of sensing sessions and on-site visits to units by senior officers so that they can personally observe the climate and talk with soldiers); and
- An expansion of emotional intelligence training to officers at all levels.

Recommendations about the most effective *individual* response strategies for dealing with a situation involving a toxic leader included:
- Just "wait it out" knowing that the individual will soon be promoted;
- Use the chain of command to report abuse; avoid the toxic leader;
- Identify a person the toxic leader trusts and work through that individual;
- Make it a point to learn what *not* to do from the toxic leader;
- Communicate regularly and provide feedback intended to help the toxic leader become more self-aware of his impact on others;
- Check Army regulations to see if his actions are improper or illegal and approach the problem from that angle;
- Provide "cover" for subordinates in order to protect them;
- Teach subordinates what "good leadership" looks like and regularly practice it so that toxic behaviors are not imitated;
- File a complaint with the Inspector General; and
- Stay focused on one's underlying reasons for service to the U.S. Army—to protect the nation and the Constitution.

Limitations of the Study—This was an exploratory study. As a result, caution is advised when attempting to generalize these findings to the Army at-large or to any other organization. The findings are only suggestive and representative of a small—but important—group of military officers. Other possible limitations were also noted.

Suggestions for Future Research—It would be useful to examine the perceptions of Army officers at varying ranks (including both commissioned and non-commissioned officers) and to compare the perceptions of officers from the Air Force, Navy, and Marines. Future studies to examine the link between emotional intelligence and the use of toxic leader behaviors would be of use, both in corporate and military contexts. In addition, studies to explore whether expanded training makes any difference in future levels of negative leadership would be of interest. Other potential recommendations for future research were noted.

Originality/Value/Implications—This is one of the earliest empirical studies of its kind which directly explored the perceptions of Army officers about how they make distinctions between toxic leaders, tough bosses, and exceptional leaders in a military context.

A better understanding of these distinctions may help the Army identify toxic leaders earlier so that they can coach them to change or relieve them of command before the damage to their unit is too great. This additional clarity may also help the Army to identify and retain tough bosses who coach, mentor, and develop their subordinates while challenging them to perform at ever higher levels of excellence to accomplish the mission—which is in everyone's best interest. Improved clarity about the distinctions is also likely to help ensure that not all negative or poor leadership is categorized and mislabeled as "toxic".

The study also identified several contributing factors that may inadvertently encourage or promote the use of toxic behaviors as a leadership style. And lastly, the study yielded a number of recommended actions—both individual and systemic—that may be taken to individually respond to or organizationally address the problem of toxic leaders.

Funding for the Study—This study was funded by a faculty research grant from Sullivan University which is based in Louisville, Kentucky. The authors remain grateful for the university's support for this work.

Keywords: *toxic leaders, tough boss, toxic leadership, dark leadership, abusive supervision, bullying, destructive leadership, negative leadership, intent, bullying, toxicity, self-interest, abuse of power, personalized power orientation, socialized power orientation, emotional intelligence, command climate, U.S. Army, constructivist grounded theory*

Reference

Daniel, T.A. & Metcalf, G.S. (2015). *Crossing the line: An examination of toxic leadership in the U.S. Army* doi: 10.13140/RG.2.1.2700.4969. https://www.academia.edu/11743522/Crossing_the_Line_An_Examina tion_of_Toxic_Leadership_in_the_U_S_Army.

Appendix III
Executive Summary: A Focus on *Exceptional* Leaders

Purpose—The purpose of this phase of the study was to contribute to the future operational readiness and institutional strength of the U.S. Army by examining the perceptions of senior officers about how the core practices of exceptional leaders differ from other types of leaders, and how great leaders impact those under their command and the organization (Daniel & Metcalf, 2015).

Design/Methodology/Approach—This empirical, qualitative study engaged in the secondary analysis of an existing data set from a series of in-depth, semi-structured interviews with 44 officers of the U.S. Army. Thirty-five of the interviews took place in person or by telephone with officers attending the Command and General Staff College in Fort Leavenworth, Kansas, while nine of the interviews were conducted with other military personnel based in Kentucky who met the sample criteria. The analysis, interpretations, and conclusions about the data were conducted in accord with the constructivist, grounded theory methodology outlined by Charmaz (2006), using constant comparative analysis.

Findings—All of the participants (100%) could identify one or more leaders who they perceived to be "exceptional". The data provided evidence that good/tough leaders and exceptional leaders are virtually identical in their use of these core practices:
- They care about their soldiers (e.g., get to know them on a personal basis, are compassionate, supportive and approachable, and they pay attention to the impact of work on both the soldier and his family);
- They develop their soldiers (e.g., mentor and coach regularly, offer honest and constructive feedback, communicate openly and frequently, allow "freedom to maneuver" and provide both family and career counseling);
- Moreover, they exhibit high levels of emotional intelligence (e.g., they are empathetic, calm under pressure, they establish a climate of mutual trust and respect, they really listen, and they are highly self-aware of their impact on others);
- They are intensely focused on mission accomplishment (e.g., lead from the front, have high standards for self and others, and exhibit a "tough but fair" approach); and
- They lead with tomorrow in mind (e.g., make decisions that are in the long-term best interests of the organization).

The new theory which emerged from the data is that great leaders are distinguished from other types of leaders by their ***highly personalized caring***. The relationships that they establish with people under their command goes beyond just showing con-

https://doi.org/10.1515/9783111201771-019

cern. They succeed in creating a positive command climate and accomplish the mission by maintaining Army values and by caring and connecting with their people in a deeply personal way (through mentoring, counseling, coaching, and frequent two-way communication). Moreover, their intense focus on their people creates high levels of mutual trust, makes soldiers feel genuinely valued and respected, and strengthens the organization for the long term.

Limitations of the Study—This was an exploratory study. As a result, we advise caution when generalizing these findings to the Army at-large or to any other organization. We can only indicate that our findings are suggestive and representative of a small—but important—group of mid-grade officers. Other limitations are identified and discussed as well.

Suggestions for Future Research—It would be useful to examine the perceptions of Army officers at varying ranks (including both commissioned and non-commissioned officers) and to compare the perceptions of officers from the Air Force, Navy, and Marines about the characteristics of exceptional leaders. It would also be interesting to investigate whether there are differences in the perceptions of officers based on gender, seniority, and other demographic variables of interest. Future studies to examine the link between emotional intelligence and the use of positive leader behaviors would also be of use.

Originality/Value/Implications—This empirical study directly explores the perceptions of Army officers about leaders in a military context, extending the earlier work of Ulmer, Shaler, Bullis, Snodgrass, Brockman, Jacobs, and Funk (2011). These findings may help the Army to better understand the characteristics of exceptional leaders, what they do differently from other leaders, and the impact of great leaders on both their subordinates and their organization so that those skills can be emphasized in their leadership development, coaching, and mentoring programs, and so that exceptional leaders can be recognized and rewarded appropriately.

In addition, this study also supports McClelland's theory (McClelland, 1975) that both exceptional and tough but capable leaders have a socialized power orientation given their emphasis on the development of others and their focus on the achievement of goals that will positively impact the organization for the long term.

Funding for the Study—This study was funded by a faculty research grant from Sullivan University which is based in Louisville, Kentucky. The authors remain grateful for the university's support for this work.

Keywords: *positive leadership, exceptional leaders, great leaders, tough bosses, socialized power orientation, emotional intelligence, U.S. Army, constructivist grounded theory*

References

Charmaz, K. (2006). *Constructing grounded theory: A practical guide through qualitative analysis*. Sage.

Daniel, T.A. & Metcalf, G.S. (2015). Crossing the line: An examination of toxic leadership in the U.S. Army. doi: 10.13140/RG.2.1.2700.4969. https://www.academia.edu/11743522/Crossing_the_Line_An_Examination_of_Toxic_Leadership_in_the_U_S_Army.

McClelland, D.C. (1975). *Power: The inner experience*. Irvington.

Ulmer, W.F.J., Shaler, M.D., Bullis, R.C., Snodgrass, W.M., Brockman, D., Jacobs, T.O., & Funk, P.E. (2011). *Leadership lessons at division command level-2010: A review of division commander leader behaviors and organizational climates in selected Army divisions after nine years of war*. United States War College.

Appendix IV
Comments from Study Participants about
Exceptional Leaders

Great leaders really took the time to show you what right looks like. They might have not always been you know the most how would I say fluffy, or touchy feely of people . . . I literally had a leader who explained it to me . . . as all pushing that ball uphill, it's a boulder. Some people are the feet, some people are the hands, some people are the brains, some people are the muscles but everyone has to contribute, therefore we push the machine uphill.

What's most common I think is that ability to establish trust between themselves and their subordinates. I used to call it compassion in leadership before I was, really, I think taught some of the more formal terms for it . . . who were approachable, who demonstrate that they really cared about the welfare of the individual so that's where when people say is it mission first or men first you get the response it's mission first, men [soldiers] always.

I've really had two exceptional leaders that I thought were just outstanding . . . One of the things that I really learned here at school is about mission command and really being able to trust leaders . . . I was in a position of responsibility within those two organizations with these two leaders and even though I was young in that certain position they were able to trust me and then help guide me through what I needed to do to make the organization successful.

So really the biggest thing is that trust factor, allowing your subordinates to take an idea, run with it and kind of that decentralized execution portion of mission command . . . I guess what we call EI or EQ to be able to see that in subordinates and say, "Okay, this is what he needs now and this is what he needs, this type of mentorship is what he needs at this point in time in his career or at this point in time in this problem that we're solving or at this other problem that we're dealing with this is the type of mentorship that he needs."

One of the best leaders I've ever had, he was very empowering, he was very kind, he was genuine, he would tell you his expectations and he would tell you immediately if you were meeting them or not meeting them but he never did it in a judgmental way . . . You could tell that he actually cared about people and he didn't just pretend. He actually said less about how much he cared about you than any of the other leaders I ever had, but you knew that he did care about you.

He cared for all of us, for the soldiers, for the officers, he took time out of his day to go around and check and see how we were doing and would take time in tasks he would

https://doi.org/10.1515/9783111201771-020

give us instead of just saying do this and get it done when you would bring it back he would coach you through it, he would talk to you about some of the things and ask you what problems you had along the way. He was what I would think as also a good inspirational leader so he knew how to really reach out, reach the core of leadership . . . And those were really the things that stood out most to me is that he cared and that he was able to inspire and motivate us to do things.

He was really in to make sure that, you know, as Lieutenants we actually knew our job. I mean not only just you know not just you're technical aspect of your job whatever but what you need to do to actually be good soldiers and stuff and not only that part too but also your family life.

Trust is big; basically trusting me to do my job and then at the same time knowing that I'm going to trust them to do their job. Not just allow me to go do my job but making sure I had the tools and resources, the training to do my job. Communication is very important as well, basically be clear, concise with what they wanted me to do and then making sure that I understood I knew their intent and then not only that just personal skills, you know yeah most of it was interaction about the job but still getting to know me for who I was, whether it's talking about sports or whatever it is so that way I'm not just a number . . . This individual you know he wouldn't ever curse at you, if he was mad, he wouldn't belittle you or degrade you but he would be like well we need to work more on this or we need to get a little bit better with this. So all of those things were very important.

A leader I thought was really good, really focused on what the unit needed as a whole, I guess you would say created a vision. Spent a lot of time getting that to be a joint vision and spent a lot time communicating with his leaders in a leadership within the unit to help drive that common goal . . . . He was personable, he was intelligent. I also enjoyed the fact that it seemed like whenever there was a problem situation something went wrong he didn't seem to lash out. [Instead], he seemed to step back and say, "Let's think about it, let's discuss it, okay now let's talk about it, let's figure out what happened." Not that someone wouldn't necessarily get in trouble, but he tried to approach it from a more thought out perspective instead of just an initial reaction to something.

The core is a sense of empathy but not just an "oh come in my office cry on my shoulder" but just an ability to actually communicate with other individuals and be able to see things from their perspective and understand where all the parties are coming from.

It's not so much the specific things that he did but rather I think the thing that really caught me and caught a lot of the officers in the organization was the climate that just not really it wasn't the physical presence of where we were at you know that wasn't a very nice area but rather the net environment of the job that we went to everyday was very inviting. It was not the hit the nail, it wasn't a feeling of despair when you went to work. People actually wanted to go to work and do a good job because we knew that we were part of a team and what we did mattered . . . He fostered that in a way, the way that he led but mostly the way that he empowered his subordinates to do their job. I think that was really a better – not as physical place because we worked ourselves to death but we did it knowing that it was for something better than ourselves . . .

He had individual conversations with us. He would field our problems. He wouldn't wait for the brigade or battalion commander to come around and let him know he would just go direct to that person and follow up with a discussion so the squadron commander, battalion commander, the XO for that unit . . . letting us do our jobs and being very flexible when it came to that sort of thing. That is kind of actually the whole idea behind why he was a good leader and how it did provide a good leadership . . . His command philosophy, his objectives for the deployment to train them, were all very clearly articulated so communication is probably a big part of the success achieved and a substantial instrument. That's just about it, trust, communication, he's got a nice commander philosophy up front and then he would just give us the baton and let us operate.

I think probably what I appreciated about them the most was their ability to stay calm under pressuring circumstances. They were able to see the big picture and I would say the long picture. So I guess they'd encountered enough situations in their careers that worked out that they could see and keep things in perspective . . . I think mostly just calm under fire and very intelligent and have the ability to kind of bring out the best in me . . . Their desire to mentor as well – they actually took the time to ask me how I was doing, how my family was doing, and then just gave me things to think about for the future. It wasn't always just current mission focus but it was what are you thinking about doing next? They would kind of link me up with people that could possibly assist me in my goals.

He was one of those leaders that took you out of your comfort zone, made you strive for excellence and you know if you tripped he might you know kind of give you a little bit of a spanking it was not you're terrible I'm going to end your career type it was hey you've made a mistake I'm going to help you improve yourself and he took a personal effort for all the leaders but especially the company commanders which were two levels below him. He really focused on getting company commanders to better themselves and I think it was because he knew that you know everything kind of floated around company commander so if he made company commanders better the unit as a whole would excel and you know he wanted to be successful in our mission.

A great leader, first of all, sets a command climate that's open that allows interchange of ideas. You understand that eventually the buck stops with that person but that's often about the pros and cons of decisions being made as time permits. Then they're also very honest and they're forthcoming and they're open. They don't hide things from you. They don't keep things close to the chest. You're not trying to always figure out where you stand. They make it clear where you stand. They create fair if sometimes demanding requirements of you but they link it back to the mission or the vision they create. The best leaders are those that have a vision, they can give vision to adequately describe it to you, get you to buy into it and then you want to help complete that vision because you own a piece of it. And finally those leaders that set an example for you and where the care results at a fitness level, their character and other things that are kind of tangible and intangible about the way you see a person.

He was one of those that, you know, they led from the front; in other words for example we had a leak in the barracks where we stayed, he came in, he called people, they couldn't get there for a while so he was right there with us rolling up his sleeves in his uniform and grabbed a mop and a mop bucket and started helping fix up. So he was one of those that, you know, even though he was in a leadership position he would not ask anything of you that he would not ask of himself, also very intelligent, very compassionate, but also very tough . . . There was really no hidden agenda and he always fought for the soldiers, in other words, he was not afraid to go up against other senior leaders if he thought it was best for the soldiers that he did.

The guy was kind. He listened to what we had to say, always made up his mind after hearing both sides of the story and everybody was happy working for him.

Every one of them demonstrated well what we used to know in the old school as being a new mentality of leadership. They lived the example we're supposed to so you know they weren't, they didn't tell you something to do that they haven't done before or that was unrealistic, but they were all very I wouldn't say rigid, they were very structured, loved what they did, and they were fair.

It was an environment where you wanted to come to work. You didn't mind getting up in the morning and putting on your boots and coming in and executing your function and not only did you know did you not have a problem about coming in you wanted to. [What made them exceptional was that they gave you] J-1: Freedom of maneuver. Management, but not micromanagement. Counseling but not belittling . . . positive feedback. You know positive, constructive criticism instead of destructive criticism . . .

Reference

Excerpted from Daniel, T.A. & Metcalf, G.S. (2015). Crossing the line: *An examination of toxic leadership in the U.S. Army*. doi: 10.13140/RG.2.1.2700.4969. https://www.academia.edu/11743522/Crossing_the_Line_An_Examination_of_Toxic_Leadership_in_the_U_S_Army.

Disclaimer

The information contained in this book is for informational purposes only and not for the purpose of providing legal advice. You should contact your attorney to obtain advice with respect to any particular issue or problem, including making revisions or updates to your policies, processes, and procedures.

Use of and access to this book does not create an attorney-client relationship between the author and the user. Lastly, the author bears the sole responsibility for the contents of this book, as well as for the underlying research study which serves as its foundation. The discussions and opinions contained herein do not necessarily reflect the views of her collaborator, research assistants, Sullivan University, the study's participants, or the employees, officers, or directors of the Sullivan University System.

https://doi.org/10.1515/9783111201771-021

About the Author

Teresa A. Daniel, JD, PhD serves as Dean and Professor – Human Resource Leadership Programs at Sullivan University (www.sullivan.edu) based in Louisville, KY. She is also the Chair for the HRL concentration in the university's PhD in Management program.

Dr. Daniel has a significant body of research in HR with an emphasis on two primary areas of inquiry: (1) *counterproductive work behaviors* (focused on workplace bullying, sexual harassment, and toxic leadership), and (2) *HR's unique role and its impact on organizational effectiveness* (primarily in the management of toxic workplace emotions, responding to situations of workplace bullying and harassment, dealing with toxic leaders, building positive work cultures, and the management of people during mergers and acquisitions). She provides consulting services focused on these topics at InterConnections LLC (www.inter connectionsllc.com).

Dr. Daniel's research has been actively supported by the national Society for Human Resource Management (SHRM) through the publication of numerous articles, interviews, and two books. Her most recent book is *Organizational toxin handlers: The critical role of HR, OD, and coaching practitioners in managing toxic workplace situations* (Palgrave Macmillan, 2020). She is also the co-author of two books with Dr. Gary Metcalf titled *Stop bullying at work: Strategies and tools for HR, legal & risk management professionals* (SHRM, 2016, 2009) and *The management of people in mergers & acquisitions* (Quorum Books, 2001), as well as numerous research studies, conference presentations, workshops, book chapters, and articles.

Dr. Daniel was honored as an Initial Fellow of the *International Academy on Workplace Bullying, Mobbing, and Abuse* in 2014 and received the *Distinguished Alumnus Award* at Centre College in 2002. She was the 2019 Grand Prize Winner of the national *SHRM HR Haiku* contest. She can be reached via email at tdaniel@sullivan.edu or TeresaAnnDaniel@gmail.com.

https://doi.org/10.1515/9783111201771-022

Index

https://doi.org/10.1515/9783111201771-023